THE DUNGEON OF THE HEART

THE MACMILLAN COMPANY
NEW YORK • CHICAGO
DALLAS • ATLANTA • SAN FRANCISCO
LONDON • MANILA

IN CANADA
BRETT-MACMILLAN LTD.
GALT, ONTARIO

THE
DUNGEON
OF
THE
HEART

Human Isolation and the American Novel

EDWIN T. BOWDEN

New York   The Macmillan Company   1961

First Printing

The Macmillan Company, New York
Brett-Macmillan Ltd., Galt, Ontario

Printed in the United States of America

Library of Congress catalog card number: 61–8262

As social conditions become more equal, the number of persons increases who, although they are neither rich nor powerful enough to exercise any great influence over their fellows, have nevertheless acquired or retained sufficient education and fortune to satisfy their own wants. They owe nothing to any man, they expect nothing from any man; they acquire the habit of always considering themselves as standing alone, and they are apt to imagine that their whole destiny is in their own hands.

Thus not only does democracy make every man forget his ancestors, but it hides his descendants and separates his contemporaries from him; it throws him back forever upon himself alone and threatens in the end to confine him entirely within the solitude of his own heart.

ALEXIS DE TOCQUEVILLE, *Democracy in America*, "Of Individualism in Democratic Countries" (1840)

A Word in Preface

This is a book written for anyone interested in the American novel or in the patterns of American life. It is not written exclusively for the small and learned group of professional students of literature or sociology or any of the other often restricted areas of professional academic study. A book for the professional would undoubtedly be more thoroughly documented, more carefully bolstered with the conclusions of other scholars, and perhaps more rigorously argued. The subject of the theme of human isolation in the American novel is fruitful enough to deserve that sort of treatment too. But I have in mind that ideal general reader—who may be a student or a professional also—who wants to hear discussed some of the great American novels, who is curious about the American mind and its history in the past, and who is interested in the relationship between those novels and that American life. I will settle for less but hope for all. There is growing now in the academic world a serious attempt to correlate all knowledge about America in one formal area of academic study. In so far as that attempt does represent a real interest on the part of Americans, it suggests the sort of reader that I have tried to satisfy. Yet I must confess that my own personal interests are primarily in American literature—I am even, I hurriedly admit, one of those professional students—and I have undoubtedly placed my greatest emphasis here on the literature as literature.

Yet my confession of interest does not, I believe, deny my first insistence that this book is not just for the student of literature. The point is that literature cannot be divorced from the real life that it reflects and represents. To know the American novel is to a large extent at least to know American life, and to know something of American life is a necessary prerequisite to understanding the American novel. I have assumed here that the reader knows something of both and is interested in pursuing the interrelationship further. The problem of human isolation is one of the great and pressing ones in American life and so is one of the great themes of the American novel. It could be pursued from either direction: its role in American intellectual and social history, and the reflection of that role in the American novel; or its thematic role in the novel, and the relationship of that role to American life or American history. Because of my personal interest, I have chosen to pursue the second possibility.

To make my point, I have chosen twelve novels that can well represent the best that have been written in America. Most of them are famous novels, and reams of critical writing on each are available in any library. Although I have gone through a large part of this criticism at one time or another, I have resisted the temptation to refer to it here. The professional will know when I am in agreement and when I am in disagreement with others, and the general reader will not care. I will only say that my discussion of the theme of isolation in the novels is my own, although inevitably some aspects of it in the various novels have been touched on here and there before. I have chosen famous novels and have restricted my discussion to them not only because they represent the best but because they also are the most familiar. I have tried as I go along to offer enough of an indirect summary of each to jog the hazy memory of the reader who may have read the novel some time ago, but each discussion is based on the assumption that the novel has at least been read at some time. If the reader does not know the one at hand, he can skip over that discussion or he can read on through it in the hope— at least it is my hope—that it will make him want to read the novel itself.

The discussion of each individual novel is for the most part gathered together at one point in the book. I have done that in order to give the book a double usefulness, first as a longer and more general discussion of the whole theme of isolation in the American novel, and second as a series of particular discussions of particular novels. I have found in my own reading that often after going through a critical work I will, perhaps some time later, want to come back to see what it has to say about one author or one novel. Then I do not want to have to hunt laboriously through a whole series of references scattered through the book. And so this book may be read as one connected whole or as a series of more or less self-contained discussions. In a sense the book has two interrelated subjects: the theme as a theme, and the novels in which the theme is presented. The two cannot, of course, be separated, but they can provide two methods of organization of the discussion that may each have its own usefulness.

By concentrating on the theme of isolation in each novel, I have necessarily limited the discussion of that novel. These are all rich and provocative novels that might each require a whole book to itself for a complete critical discussion. But the discussion even limited to the theme of isolation has proved enlightening for me at least. For one reason, any different way of looking at a great work is itself likely to be interesting and to lead to new insights. In examining the complexity of a really first-rate novel, it is convenient to have a standpoint from which to observe and to orient oneself, and a new light thrown even experimentally on a novel may often bring out shades and forms unnoticed before. For another, the theme of isolation is so central to these works, so important in what they are trying to do, that it leads to understanding of each novel as a whole rather than simply to one or two of its elements. An examination of a particular theme then becomes a sort of critical can opener that exposes the whole book to view—or perhaps to consumption. Once opened, the novel may then be consumed at leisure by the reader. The theme works this well for the critic because it is not an idea—or a light, to mix the metaphor still further—brought from outside but one found as an organic element of the novels themselves. In a real sense the theme *is* the novels and so naturally carries the critic into the full content of each one. The subject is not an artificial one but an integral and an enlightening view drawn out of the novels themselves. I hope that the reader will go on to expand the view for himself, both within the individual novel and in the whole broad area of the relationship of the novel to the American scene of its particular time and of our present time as well. The theme of human isolation belongs equally to both.

American publishers always deserve thanks for the use of copyright material from their books, and I gladly extend thanks here. On first quotation from any book I have given a full bibliographical reference, including name of publisher, to the first American edition, the text that I have used consistently for quotation. The Humanities Research Center of the University of Texas furnished these often rare editions.

I would especially like to take the opportunity here to acknowledge the gifts of time and support offered by the University of Texas while I wrote this book. If it were not for grants from the University Research Institute of the University of Texas I would still be hunting and pecking and looking vainly for an unclaimed hour or two. Of course if there had not been my children, Elisabeth, Susan, and Edwin Eric, there might have been a few more hours, but who would want hours at that expense? As for Ann—she is proof that the heart need never be a dungeon after all. To the four of them I dedicate this book.

EDWIN T. BOWDEN
Austin, 1960

Contents

I

Introduction:
Sweet and Delightful Society

It is an inevitable fact that the literature of a country reflects something of the life of the country. This book is a discussion of twelve great American novels that reflect the continuing concern in American life with the problem of human isolation. They hardly include all of the great American novels, of course, although it would be difficult to make a list that does not include a fair number of them. They are not all great novels either, I suppose, if the most stringent requirements for greatness are invoked. But they do at least represent the best that the novel has produced in this country, and it is a best of which Americans can be proud. The interesting point in common—and it is one shared with a great many other novels that do not appear here—is that all are concerned in large degree with the subject of human isolation in America, the loneliness of man separated from his fellow man and the resulting effect on the life or mind or emotions of the American caught up in the problem. They do not each present the same situation and certainly do not all agree on the answer to the problem, although there is in the end a surprising agreement on certain general principles. They are simply—or rather, not so simply—the result of a dozen novelists' thoughts about a problem that has always concerned the American and so has always furnished a subject for the American novelist.

It would be misleading to discuss these novels as though human isolation has concerned only the American. Many of the great European novels have taken up the theme; Cervantes in his *Don Quixote*, the father of all of our modern novels, made it an original part of the tradition of the novel. As the literary historian glances down the list of great European novels many with similar themes jump to mind: Flaubert's *Madame Bovary*, for instance, or Dostoevsky's *Crime and Punishment*. The English novel has in general not been quite so concerned with the lonely man, although Richardson in *Clarissa*, the mother of the English novel if not the father, introduced the theme in one form, and the modern novelists, in such works as Joyce's *Portrait of the Artist as a Young Man*, have taken it up again in another form. Perhaps it is inevitable that the novel should present the theme often, for loneliness and isolation have always been problems of the human being everywhere. Then, too, the novel by its very nature tends to concentrate on a few characters and to isolate them in order to gain intensity and familiarity, even though the sprawling extension and the wide range of characters of the English eighteenth and nineteenth century novel may have prevented it from being devoted to the theme quite so often as the Continental novel.

Many of the great novels, too, have been at least partially tragic in nature or in effect. Just why is an interesting source of speculation, although the speculation will eventually lead one around again to the subject of human isolation. For isolation in its omnipresent nature is often one of the sources of tragedy and is always one of its elements. There can be no complete tragedy when the individual has large gifts of aid and comfort and strength and understanding from without. There can be sorrow and hurt but never complete tragedy in any meaningful sense. The great tragedies of the modern world have understood this fact and to gain the desired effect in their world of imagination have isolated their tragic heroes. Hamlet, for instance, gradually finds himself surrounded only by treacherous or corrupt or stupid characters who force him more and more into the shell of his own isolation. Even Horatio, the one possible source of understanding and sympathy, does not quite understand Hamlet or what is going on about him. Hamlet must at last face fate and his opponents alone and unaided. King Lear, the archetype of the tragic man in English tragedy, sees—or at least thinks he sees—all of his daughters turn against him, his retainers taken away, his friends banished. In the storm on the heath he must face the elements and stand up against the world and confront himself alone, accompanied only by the fool who taunts him with his isolation. When at last he finds too late that Cordelia does love him, that the world is not, after all, made up of separate and hostile identities, he can die with a smile, for his tragic ordeal is over. The loss of the sense of separation has meant the finding of peace again. These great tragedies of the past are archetypal: as the drama in English began to give way in energy and effect to the novel, the novel inevitably continued the same pattern of isolated hero in its particular form of the tragedy, whether a full-scale tragedy or more simply a story with tragic elements or implications.

The novel, then, European or American, has consistently made use of the isolated character demanded by the literary form itself or by the seemingly inevitable tragic implications. The American novel, however, has made particularly strong and insistent use, enough so that isolation may be fairly called a common theme of American fiction. For, more often than in the European novel, the American novel does not simply make use of the isolated man; it is *about* the isolated man and about isolation itself. The dozen representative novels discussed here form together an extended

essay on isolation in America, a finer and more immediate
essay than any philosophical or historical disquisition might
be. That is not to say for a moment that these novels are
long essays disguised as fiction; the relationship between the
theme and the story is far more complex. Certainly the
theme or the "essay" grows out of the story and the charac-
terization rather than the other way round. That is, the
story is not there to illustrate the idea; rather the idea is
suggested by the story. And the suggestion is generally conveyed by implication, by analogy, by a sort of pervasive
dramatic presence rather than by direct and obvious statement by the author speaking in his own voice. It is up to the
reader, then, to catch the implications and to interpret the
story. This book is aimed at helping the reader do just that.
It is very doubtful that the author wrote the particular novel
under discussion with any clear intention of commenting on
the problem of isolation in America. The theme was simply
one that caught his imagination, consciously or unconsciously,
and worked itself out in dramatic form in a story. In effect,
the story is the theme and the theme is the story; the two are
so synonymous that they cannot be discussed separately. In
fact they are not two at all but one unity that can occasionally be discussed as though there were two parts involved.
But whatever the intention of the various authors here—and
trying to decide seems a pointless endeavor—the fact is that
all are presenting some aspect of the same, constantly recur-
ring theme.

The theme is there, of course, because it represents a
problem or challenge in American life itself: the sense of
separation from civilization or from home or from accepted
ideas and familiar ways or, most strongly, from fellow
beings; in short, the sense of isolation. The historian or the
sociologist might make it his business to trace the history of
isolation in America and to define it for particular times and

conditions. But the novel does it just as well, although more indirectly, and in some ways does it better, for the novel at its best lets the reader see and know believable people— even though imaginary—caught up in the historical—and far from imaginary—fact. As Henry James pointed out in one of the most incisive essays written on the novel, *The Art of Fiction*, it is the business of the novel just as much as of history to represent life directly and to illustrate the actions of men. Even a summary glance at the social and intellectual history of America reveals the times and the occasions and the conditions with which the novel is concerned.

The American frontier, of course, is the most obvious physical condition of isolation, and the historians since Frederick Jackson Turner have taught us to see the importance of the frontier in shaping American thought. Cooper's Leatherstocking tales in the early nineteenth century and Willa Cather's novels in the early twentieth are immediately relevant. But the history of the frontier with its characteristic lonely battle of man against his environment and against himself is only a representative of so much of American history.

From the first landing of the Pilgrims the characteristic American experience and challenge have been of human isolation. The predominant religious history, for instance— illustrated by almost any of the literature of early New England—has been that of the search by the individual for some immediate private relationship with God, and then the search for a church that will preserve this sense of private relationship within the larger religious community. The man who can find neither or only one is likely to end a lonely man—or perhaps the founder of a new sect.

In one sense even the political history has been in keeping, for it has seen and continues to see the struggle of the individual to gain recognition and acceptance as an isolated entity in the political group. Here the "political novels" of the twentieth century gain much of their impact. Some people want to lose themselves in the group, others to maintain a strict individual isolation; but whatever their personal position, Americans have always sought the public right of individual isolation as well as the public right of group union.

Most immediately relevant to the novel, however, is what might be called the social or even the psychological history of America, the struggle of the individual mind to preserve its isolated identity within the security of society. Most of the great American novels place their theme of isolation within this general area. And rightly so, for this is the ground on which Americans have most often had to fight their individual battles and make their separate peace. It is with this general area, too, that our present civilization is most concerned. Two recent very popular and influential books point up the concern. *The Lonely Crowd* (1950) by David Riesman with Nathan Glazer and Reuel Denney presents the hypothesis that Americans are changing from "inner-directed" people, who find the authority originally derived from adult teaching now within themselves, to "other-directed" people, who derive their authority from the example of the crowd about them. *The Organization Man* (1956) by William H. Whyte, Jr., demonstrates the present tendency of many Americans to subordinate their individual personality to the security of "the organization," to take their direction cheerfully and willingly from their group life—the business corporation, the government, the union, the university—rather than from their own "inner-direction." These books and others like them are interesting and provocative—and sometimes a little frightening. But they are simply saying about their time what the American novel has been saying about its various times from the beginning.

The times and the problems have varied, of course, over the century and a half that the novel has been a major form in America. If J. D. Salinger's *The Catcher in the Rye* (1951), in agreement with Riesman and Whyte, presents an argument against conformity to the organized life, Steinbeck's *Grapes of Wrath* (1939) presents an argument for the necessity of belonging to the group. If Cooper's *The Deerslayer* (1841), written at a time of growing industrialism, holds up in nostalgia a romantic picture of isolation in the forest, Howells' *The Rise of Silas Lapham* (1885), written at the full growth of the new big business, pictures a man who finds that he cannot deny the moral demands of business in uncommitted isolation.

Wide reading in the novel is the equivalent of wide reading in the social history of America; and reading that has something of the double value of good historical writing: it presents the history itself, the truthful account of times and people, and it presents the author's interpretation of that account, the play of his intelligence over the raw material. In the vocabulary of the literary critic the novel can present characters and a story and a background that grow from the truth of times and people, but it can also present a theme, a concept—even a doctrine—that grows from the intelligence and the convictions of the author playing over that story. Most of the great American novels are united in this way to American life, and in one manner or another lead the reader back to that very real life. The novel has grown from American history and has become a form of history in itself.

The novel springs so directly from the truth of American life that one of America's first great histories seems a fitting introduction to the theme of human isolation even in the novel. Governor William Bradford's *History of Plymouth Plantation* is particularly fitting too for it gives something of the effect of a novel itself: it tells a good story against a believable background; it presents interesting people and does not hesitate to develop their character by anecdote and illustration; it maintains its unity by an organic relevance of the parts rather than by mere chronological sequence; it has an imaginative quality in the emotional and intellectual impact of its details as well as in its broad sweep; it develops a number of themes by dramatization and by implication as well as by explicit statement. In short, it is first-rate historical writing and so has by nature much in common with the novel. But, more important here, one of the major themes it presents as it considers even the very earliest life in America is the theme of human isolation in the New World. It is too bad that in the seventeenth century the novel had not yet appeared (even though the Puritans would certainly have rejected it if it had existed), for it would be interesting to see what themes it had in common with Bradford's history. Undoubtedly one would have been the theme of isolation, for Bradford makes clear that isolation was one of the great and troublesome problems in early American life.

"Being thus passed the vast ocean, and a sea of troubles before in their preparation . . . , they had now no friends to welcome them nor inns to entertain or refresh their weatherbeaten bodies; no houses or much less towns to repair to, to seek for succour." So Governor Bradford in his manuscript history *Of Plymouth Plantation* begins his description of the condition of the Pilgrims on their first landing at Plymouth in the new country.

Besides, what could they see but a hideous and desolate wilderness, full of wild beasts and wild men—and what multitudes there might be of them they knew not. Neither could they, as it were, go up to the top of Pisgah, to view from this wilderness a more goodly country to feed their hopes; for which way soever they turned their eyes (save upward to the heavens) they could have little solace or content in respect of any outward objects.

Before them only a wilderness; behind, "there was the mighty ocean which they had passed and was now as a main bar and

gulf to separate them from all the civil parts of the world."
The conclusion is inevitable and moving: "What could now
sustain them but the Spirit of God and His grace?" [62–63] [1]
With this passage the greatness of American literature began,
and with it too began the theme of human isolation that has
run through the history of America's literature.

The experience of physical isolation on the frontier was
to be repeated over and over again in the American experience. From Plymouth north to Maine, south to Texas, west
to California and Oregon, up into Alaska, Americans were
to find themselves facing a wilderness, cut off from the aid
and comfort of the civilization left behind, thrown upon
their own material and spiritual resources. The wilderness
hunters, the frontier farmers, the Indian fighters, the gold
seekers all found themselves in somewhat the same position
as the small band landing from the *Mayflower*, however
much different historical circumstances and the passage of
time may have altered the aims and assumptions of these later
men. For the problem is inherent in the American experience,
perhaps because of the continued lack of settled community
and accepted tradition in a new and expanding country.
The American has always been sensitive to the threat and
the promise of human isolation and the loneliness that may
or may not come with it, and in turn has made it a part of
his history, his thought, his emotions, his expression.

The shock of isolation on the shores of Plymouth was
only a moment of recognition of a physical state that had
been prefigured for the little group of Puritans—good Englishmen who had never faced a real wilderness before—by a
period of exile in a spiritual wilderness. Bradford takes exile
and persecution as a deliberate theme for the period before
the Plymouth exodus (and "exodus" is the expression for the

[1] Page references are to William Bradford, *Of Plymouth Plantation 1620–
1647*, ed. Samuel E. Morison (New York: Alfred A. Knopf, 1952).

flight that had emotional value to these early dissenters).
Even in early exile under Queen Mary the "true professors"—
those who "laboured to have the right worship of God and
discipline of Christ established in the church, according to
the simplicity of the gospel, without the mixture of men's
inventions; and to have and to be ruled by the laws of God's
Word" [6]—were persecuted by those who "endeavoured to
have the episcopal dignity (after the popish manner)" [6]
as well as by the crown. With the return to England under
Elizabeth the persecution continued, with those of the state
church "beguiling some and corrupting others till at length
they began to persecute all the zealous professors in the land
. . . both by word and deed, if they would not submit to
their ceremonies and become slaves to them and their popish
trash." [7] As time passed troubles worsened. Those of
the true church were "hunted and persecuted on every side,
so as their former afflictions were but as flea-bitings in comparison of these which now came upon them." [10] The
only solution was exile, and as every American schoolboy
knows, Holland was a temporary refuge until the final flight
to America.

As if the physical isolation of the wilderness were not
enough, the feeling of rejection and betrayal by those at
home continued for the new exiles. A great part of Bradford's
history is devoted to discussion of the wrangles with friends
and acquaintances left behind. Misunderstandings and dis-
agreements with the "adventurers" or investors who in part
financed the early settlement were in the natural order of
affairs, and Bradford reports them with a reasonable detachment. But in recounting the plots and selfish or dishonest
dealings of those supposed friends at home he writes in barely
restrained anger and hurt:

Thus all their hopes in regard of Mr. Weston were laid in the
dust; and all his promised help turned into an empty advice,

which they apprehended was neither lawful nor profitable for them to follow. And they were not only thus left destitute of help in their extreme wants, having neither victuals nor anything to trade with; but others prepared and ready to glean up what the country might have afforded for their relief. [107]

If Bradford seems at times unduly suspicious or sensitive— although he usually cites good authority for his accusations— it is for understandable reasons. It is clear that the exiles were indeed either abandoned by most of those at home, used for selfish purposes, or at best treated with unforgivable careless- ness and contempt. More than the ocean separated the little band from those it had once known and trusted, and separa- tion, as Bradford discovered, can lead to greater and greater isolation. At Plymouth the Pilgrims were soon forced to build a palisade about their settlement; it took no longer to discover the greater palisade that others were erecting about the new exiles.

Although the little group of "zealous professors" was cut off from the old country and the old society, it would be a grave misunderstanding to think of them as lonely or as isolated within themselves individually. For much of their strength, and ultimately their success, came from an unshaken sense of the mutual social covenant in which they had pledged themselves. John Robinson, the early spiritual leader of the group, had pointed out the advantage and the comfort of the covenant in a letter that Bradford reproduces:

"And the better much when you shall enjoy the presence and help of so many godly and wise brethren, for the bearing of part of your burthen, who also will not admit into their hearts the least thought of suspicion of any the least negligence, at least presumption, to have been in you, whatsoever they think in others." [367]

Whatever trials came their way—exile, starvation, disease, attack, treachery—those within the covenant knew that they had the trust and reliance of the others, and were able mutually to meet and overcome any threat of the world or of the devil. The isolation was from without, never from within.

The ultimate strength of the covenant, of course, was that it was not merely a social covenant or a covenant for mutual aid and protection, or even a covenant to achieve a praiseworthy and desired end, but an extension and an analogy of the covenant with God that was the center of the Puritan belief. God had made a covenant with man, so the theological belief was expressed, to offer salvation and grace to those who would receive it; man in return offered acceptance and faith. Those who had accepted through faith, and so were the elect in Calvinistic terms, were bound together in a covenant of faith and service. The mutual aid and dependence was not for its own sake but for service for God. This covenant of man, then, was a social one only in a secondary sense, although social unity was the impression it gave to those looking on from the outside. John Robinson and William Brewster in another letter come close to a definition when they point out:

"We are knit together as a body in a most strict and sacred bond and covenant of the Lord, of the violation whereof we make great conscience, and by virtue whereof we do hold ourselves straitly tied to all care of each other's good and of the whole, by every one and so mutually." [33]

With a unity derived from faith in God and directed toward the service of God an isolation imposed by mere man could be borne and even overcome, whatever the cost in human terms.

For the American Puritans the immediate service of the human covenant was the establishment of God's commonwealth in the new land. John Endicott, one of the leaders of the other group of Puritans, put the thought in a letter to Governor Bradford:

"And the same request (with you) I make unto the Lord that we may, as Christian brethren be united by a heavenly and unfeigned love, bending all our hearts and forces in furthering a work beyond our strength, with reverence and fear, fastening our eyes always on Him that only is able to direct and prosper all our ways." [223]

A common goal, a work beyond their strength then, further united the little group. And since it was a service for God, a direct fulfillment of God's will on earth, as well as a human challenge and ambition, the demand for concerted effort and mutual charity was undeniable. Behind the demand, too, was a threat, unexpressed by Bradford but stated clearly and movingly by John Winthrop in his *Modell of Christian Charity* on board the *Arbella* as the second large group of Puritans were coming to the new land. He says:

Wee must vphold a familiar Commerce together, . . . wee must delight in eache other, make others Condicions our owne reioyce together, mourne together, labour, and suffer together, allwayes haueing before our eyes our Commission and Community in the worke, our Community as members of the same body.

For if we do so, says Winthrop, the Lord will dwell with us and prosper our plantation as a model for later generations. And then comes the threat as well as the promise:

For wee must Consider that wee shall be as a Citty vpon a Hill, the eies of all people are vppon vs; soe that if wee shall deale falsely with our god in this worke we haue vndertaken and soe cause him to withdrawe his present help from vs, wee shall be made a story and a by-word through the world, we shall open the mouthes of enemies to speake euill of the wayes of god and all professours for Gods sake.[2]

[2] Reprinted in *The Puritans*, ed. Perry Miller and Thomas H. Johnson (New York: American Book Co., 1938), pp. 198–99.

There was no choice for the early Puritans; necessity, belief, hope, fear all combined to hold the group together in what Bradford calls "sweet and delightful society and spiritual comfort together in the ways of God." [17]

Since people are so sinful and fallen, the Puritans would have said, the zeal of the covenant could not last for long. There must have been a few rebellious individuals from the beginning, for Bradford's history has a constant undercurrent of criticism of "those that were close and cleaving to themselves and retired from the common good." [18] John Robinson had given early warning when he had advised the professors to " 'join common affections truly bent upon the general good, avoiding as a deadly plague of your both common and special comfort all retiredness of mind for proper advantage.' " [369] But the warning seems to have been ignored by a few at least. In the very beginning the Plymouth plantation was organized as an economic commonwealth, with property held in common and each person working for the entire group. It did not take long for the system to break down, and in 1623 each family was allowed to plant and harvest for itself. As Bradford admits, the new system was much more successful: men were willing to work harder for themselves than for the community. Before long, land was beginning to be held as private property, and the end of the commonwealth was approaching.

The end of the communal economic system was not the end of the tight community, but it was indicative of what was happening. In commenting on its early stages Bradford points out only how it refuted Plato and the other ancients. But as the physical community itself began to disband with the arrival of better times and more immigration, the indications of the disbanding of the group itself became too clear. One of the most affecting passages in Bradford's history is his lament at the end for the parent church left behind in

Plymouth as the families moved on to outlying settlements and new communities:

And thus was this poor church left, like an ancient mother grown old and forsaken of her children, though not in their affections yet in regard of their bodily presence and personal helpfulness; her ancient members being most of them worn away by death, and these of later time being like children translated into other families, and she like a widow left only to trust in God. Thus, she that had made many rich became herself poor. [334]

By the middle forties the first hard times were over, the first compact communities were divided and expanded, and the sense of indissolvable covenant was becoming an intellectual belief rather than a fact.

Something of the sense of community and interdependence continued in other forms, of course, until the present day. Even while Bradford is lamenting the loss of the church community at Plymouth he is telling of the new articles of confederation of The United Colonies of New-England. But political confederation is not the same thing as the covenant of the professors, as men were to continue to find. At the end of Bradford's history the mind goes back to a sorrowful note that Bradford later added to his transcription of the 1617 letter of Robinson and Brewster in which they define the "sacred bond and covenant." He laments the disappearance of the bond and adds:

I have been happy, in my first times, to see, and with much comfort to enjoy, the blessed fruits of this sweet communion, but it is now a part of my misery in old age, to find and feel the decay and want thereof (in a great measure) and with grief and sorrow of heart to lament and bewail the same. And for others' warning and admonition, and my own humiliation, do I here note the same. [33]

With the disappearance of the communion man was returned to his state of isolation, present or threatened. In a time of great trial it had been a source of private emotional assurance as well as of communal strength, but with the return of usual conditions man was returned to his usual state, able only to look back with longing and sorrow.

To explain the disappearance of the human covenant Bradford is sure that the "subtle serpent hath slyly wound in himself under fair pretences of necessity and the like, to untwist these sacred bonds and tie[s], and as it were insensibly by degrees to dissolve, or in a great measure to weaken, the same." [33] His remark is indicative of the sense of battle with which the Puritans approached their new land. Bradford begins his history by pointing to the continual "wars and oppositions" that Satan has "raised, maintained and continued against the Saints, from time to time, in one sort or other." [3] The trials imposed by weather, starvation, Indians, treacherous friends were but second causes, for behind them lay Satan trying to destroy God's work in the New World. And in opposition to Satan was the little army of God, united in the face of a dangerous and powerful enemy. In such desperate battle there could be no division in the ranks, no working of one soldier against another.

The Puritan army had an even more powerful leader, of course, and one that could not be defeated. All history—especially that of New England—was but a working out of his incomprehensible will. When, in the words of a modern army, things got too tough, God could always intervene to save his own:

Amidst these straits, and the desertion of those from whom they had hoped for supply, and when famine began now to pinch them sore, they not knowing what to do, the Lord (who never fails his) presents them with an occasion beyond all expectation. [110]

But God works through natural agents, and it was up to the Puritan group to do the actual fighting, however sure they might be of final victory. Once they began to lose the sense of mission and eased up on the active, conscious battle, the army, as armies will, began to fall apart. Bradford was certain that God disapproved; in 1638 an earthquake was a sure sign of his displeasure at the settlers' "shaking a-pieces and removals one from another." [302] But disapproval or not, the process of dissolution went on, to the sorrow of stalwarts like Bradford and the despair of the next generations of ministers who tried to restore the old zeal. Bradford's tone of mourning is appropriate, for his people seemed to have begun to capitulate to the forces of Satan, a greater defeat than any mere loss of community or personal communion.

And so the great experiment in Christian community, the glorious war of the saints, began to draw toward an end. And the new American, already a different man from his European contemporary, had again to face the problems of human isolation. The physical barriers remained: the great area, the scattered population, the regional and local differences of the new country, as well as the barrier of the sea between the new and the old. And increasingly the sense of covenant, the personal and religious tie between men devoted to their God and their cause, was failing to deny the possibility of emotional as well as physical isolation. Now a community could again be divided within itself, man from man, as well as from other and separate societies. American life had begun to take the form it was to continue to hold, except for the occasional temporary covenant of some other sort, until the present.

And yet the memory lingered, if not of the Puritan covenant of men, at least of the old dream and hope of men undivided among themselves, facing whatever a hostile world might bring against them. And there was validity in the dream, however impossible the permanent realization. For the American experience reflected in the American literature was that man, whatever his state of isolation, must strive toward some such solution as the first Puritans found for a few years: man joined with fellow man in the light of the truth and the right as they understand it. It is not accidental—perhaps it is inevitable—that the answer to the problem of human isolation was again and again to be a part of the particular specific answer embraced by the Puritans: forgetfulness of self, love of fellow man in the light of the love of God, united battle against evil, Christian charity in a hostile world. The Puritan answer took the special form of the covenant, although Bradford records, too, a number of instances in which the original group showed "a rare example herein of brotherly love, and Christian care" where it was not necessarily a part of their commitment. For later generations, with all the shifts of sensibility and of philosophical and theological assumptions that followed, the form was a different one. But working at its center was always the same answer, however much the individual and his society might like to deny it.

Whether the answer for imperfect man can ever be held for long is another matter. For the Puritans it could not, and in the account of the failure lies much of the emotional effect of Bradford's history. Most of the great American novels do not go on to consider this problem. The answer itself (or the failure to find it) is their climax. And it is an emotionally and rationally satisfying climax, for it has its roots in living human experience and human belief. The very consistency of the literature—written sometimes by men who consciously reject Christian thought, the greatest source of the answer—is evidence of that. And yet Bradford's history is still there and is still a valid description of a part of the American experience. Perhaps behind the American novel—so often a capturing of tragic experience—there is an even greater tragedy at work. Or perhaps Bradford is relevant here too in another way when he stresses the conviction that "a man's ways are not in his own power, but in His hands who hath the issues of life and death. Man may purpose, but God doth dispose." [180] If human history is but a long account of God's ways on earth, how can man look beyond the answer revealed to him? And who would dare say that it is finally tragic?

With Bradford's history for a starting point, both as a great example of the American concern with the problem of isolation and as one great answer to that problem, the American novel is able to pick up the theme again in the early nineteenth century and carry it on until the present day. Bradford belongs to the seventeenth century, but he deserves bearing in mind in the nineteenth and the twentieth as well. For he provides a convenient and a significant point of reference, a social and moral and spiritual answer to the very real problems raised in the theme of isolation, as well as a degree of emphasis on the theme that provides another kind of measurement. He is not so far back in time as he may seem, just as he is not so far from American imaginative fiction as he may seem. His writing shares in the common theme, and his life shared in the common experience. By glancing back occasionally while reading the novels of later years the reader is able to see how the theme has varied to fit the times and how the assumptions and experiences and concepts of later writers were to differ. But most important of all, he is able to see how Governor Bradford in the very first years of the colonies was able to define and to discuss with almost uncanny precision the problems and the solutions of human isolation in America that later generations and later writers were to rediscover for themselves again and again.

II

The Frontier Isolation

The physical isolation of the early American frontier, the pervading myth of the flight of the hunter before dreaded civilization—the very opposite of all that Bradford spoke for—has long been epitomized in the American mind by Daniel Boone. The story of his moving on westward because some damned Yankee settled within a hundred miles is part of the American myth. And the image of Daniel Boone, with characteristic vigor, refuses to remain fenced even within its own wide boundaries of "the dark and bloody ground," but has wandered directly into the main trail of the American adventure novel, leaving its footprints in the past and disappearing into the future.

That path begins, or at least one of its principal tributary paths begins, at the Leatherstocking novels of James Fenimore Cooper. Natty Bumppo, if not drawn directly from Boone, at least catches up many of the elements of the myth. He is the mighty hunter choosing the absolute freedom of the forest and avoiding the entanglements and restraints of the settled regions. He is the isolated man of the new frontier, loving his lonely life and wishing no other. He is himself the myth, the dream, the wish fulfillment of the American looking west. What his relationship to real man on a real frontier may be is another matter.

Cooper's fictional concern with the encroachment of civilization on the isolated frontiersman is seen in *The Pioneers* or *The Prairie*, particularly in the character of the squatter

Ishmael Bush, probably the clearest examples of the Leatherstocking Series. But *The Deerslayer* seems to come to grips
in a more meaningful fashion with the isolation both of the
mythical and of the real frontier. When Natty Bumppo—or
the Deerslayer or Hawkeye, the names given him in his
youth—sees a navigational quadrant brought to the wilderness by an acquaintance he mistakes it for a surveying instrument and immediately recoils at the thought of surveyors:

"I've seen all their tools, often, and wicked and heartless enough
are they, for they never come into the forest but to lead the way
to waste and destruction. . . . I fear me, after all, that Thomas
Hutter has journeyed into the wilderness with no fair intentions
towards its happiness." [I, 219] [1]

Here is the myth of Daniel Boone—not, of course, the real
Boone—speaking through Natty. But at the same time the
very real surveys of the Northwest Territory were made
during Cooper's own lifetime, and one recognizes the awareness by the American people of the disappearance and destruction of the wilderness forest and its lonely hunters.

Deerslayer's desire for the isolation of the unbroken forest
is not merely a desire to avoid civilization but a positive love
for the forest itself. Cooper begins the novel with the verse
"I love not Man the less, but Nature more," from the stanza
in *Childe Harold's Pilgrimage* beginning "There is a pleasure
in the pathless woods." He might have found similar lines in
Bryant that would equally have served the purpose. For
Deerslayer's love of the wilderness is that of the romantic; he
feels his soul go forth to this pure nature uncontaminated by
man and there find its spiritual home. Again and again through
the Leatherstocking Series the woods are called "God's
temple," and Natty goes there to worship, not "where two

[1] Page references are to [James F. Cooper], *The Deerslayer: or, The First
War-Path*, 2 vols. (Philadelphia: Lea and Blanchard, 1841).

or more are gathered together" but where he can be alone in direct communication with God. Here he finds his greatest joy and the pure fulfillment of his life and his being. As he carefully explains to Judith Hutter in the novel, farms have their uses, but what can a man find there that he cannot find in the forest?

"But where are you to find your shades, and laughing springs, and leaping brooks, and vinerable trees, a thousand years old, in a clearin'? You don't find *them*, but you find their disabled trunks, marking the 'arth like head-stones in a grave-yard. It seems to me that the people who live in such places, must be always thinkin' of their own inds, and of univarsal decay; and that, too, not of the decay that is brought about by time and natur', but the decay that follows waste and violence."

Then too, he goes on, churches are good enough, but the whole earth is a church.

"Moreover, all is contradiction in the settlements, while all is concord in the woods. Forts and churches almost always go together, and yet they're downright contradictions; churches being for peace, and forts for war. No, no—give me the strong places of the wilderness, which is the trees, and the churches, too, which are arbours raised by the hand of natur'." [I, 262–63]

To support such an emotion Cooper has provided Lake Glimmerglass, the Otsego of fact, as a setting for *The Deerslayer*, and it is one that both explains Deerslayer's feeling and gives it substance and form. As Deerslayer himself exclaims, " 'This *is* a sight to warm the heart! . . . the lake seems made to let us get an insight into the noble forests; and land and water, alike, stand in the beauty of God's providence!' " [I, 33] For the lake is perfect wilderness beauty, still alone and unexploited even years after the end of the events of the novel. Even Hutter's cabin, built on piles out in the water, is only a temporary perch that cannot stand there for long. But during the course of the novel the cabin as the center of events is a center of physical isolation in the lake. Here is the familiar American dream of the deserted island set in the deserted wilderness. Isolation in its desirable sense could go no further. If the term were not so foreign to Cooper's methods, Lake Glimmerglass could be called a symbol of Deerslayer's dreams, for the little lake catches up the beauty of the forest and the wilderness life and provides within itself an escape from man, Indian or white, with all his schemes and his hostility. Quite literally its mirrorlike surface reflects the heavens and the earth about it, and its surrounding hills echo the sounds of man and nature. Like Thoreau's Walden Pond, Glimmerglass brings all nature to a focus and a center, and that center for Cooper is in the lonely wilderness.

A romantic love of unspoiled nature and a desire to escape the ravages of man, however, are hardly enough to make Deerslayer a character of permanent interest. For man, however isolated, must eventually deal with man, and it is here that the deeper interest of the theme of isolation must lie. And it is here that Deerslayer captures our interest as well as our imagination. In part the novel is a love story—Cooper could seldom resist the sentimental novel of love—and there Deerslayer successfully defends his lonely bachelor state. In the next Leatherstocking novel, *The Pathfinder*, he is momentarily to put that state in jeopardy, although in not very serious jeopardy, as he proposes to a girl who is inevitably to refuse him. But here in *The Deerslayer* he must fend off Judith Hutter, who with an abandon ordinarily denied a girl in a sentimental novel proposes to him directly. He refuses her gently but almost as easily as he refuses to marry into the Mingo tribe to save his own scalp. It is fitting, of course, that he should, and in keeping with his character, for Deerslayer must remain the mythical wilderness man apart from his fellow beings except for occasional friendships and passing understandings.

At one point Cooper speaks of a "community of character" [II, 97] between the various persons of the novel. But this community is one in which Deerslayer plays little part. Tom Hutter and his two daughters are part of a family; Hurry Harry loves Judith Hutter; Judith loves Deerslayer; Chingachgook and Wah-ta-Wah are in love; only Deerslayer is unable to join in some form of love that would bind him to fellow human beings. He and Chingachgook are companions on the trail, of course, and hold a certain affection as well as mutual understanding. But Deerslayer's careful and constant distinction between "white nature" and "red nature" prevents the friendship from becoming anything more. He feels too sharply his position and his "gifts" as a white man ever to abandon or to compromise them to a red man. As he states with pride to the Mingos, what allegiance he can allow himself belongs to the Delawares, but at best it is a sympathy and a rational approval, for he himself is white. This insistence, however, places Deerslayer in an even more isolated position, for the whites of the novel, with the possible exception of the feeble-minded Hetty Hutter, are all ones for whom he can feel little sympathy or approval. For him the only wholly deserving character of the novel is Chingachgook, and he is separated by the unbridgeable gulf of "nature."

Physically and emotionally, then, Deerslayer is separated from mankind. Spiritually his position is little different. For one of Deerslayer's strongest characteristics is his constant awareness of the moral law under which he lives: " 'I know we live in the woods, Hurry, and are thought to be beyond human laws—and perhaps we are so, in fact, whatever it may be in right—but there is a law, and a law maker, that rule across the whole continent. He that flies in the face of either,

need not call me fri'nd.' " [I, 26] Duty to the moral law and
duty to the law of nature are the stern guides of this woodsman, and he interprets his duty with a strictness and a literalness that suggest the Protestant—one is tempted to say Puritan
—ethic at its shallowest and most external. And once again
he finds himself alone except for the rather dubious company
of the feeble-minded Hetty. No one else in the novel can or
will live up to his standard, and so, as he says—with an irony
probably unnoticed by Cooper himself—no one need call him
friend. He is a tower of righteousness in the wilderness, but
a tower that can only be looked up to and regarded with
awe. As Judith says, " 'It is a hard thing to fear truth, Hetty,
. . . and yet do I more dread Deerslayer's truth, than any
enemy! One cannot tamper with such truth—so much honesty—such obstinate uprightness!' " [II, 47] Obstinate uprightness of Deerslayer's sort may carry a neat lesson for
young readers, but it hardly brings the character into sympathetic relationship with erring mankind.

   The pity is that in *The Deerslayer* Natty is brought into
relationship with the erring Judith Hutter, the beautiful
young girl and sentimental heroine of the novel, and the
result is that the novel is a finer one than Cooper ever allowed
himself to know. For Judith, in one sense at least, is as isolated as Deerslayer himself. But rather than separated by a
sense of righteousness, she is separated by a sense of sin.
Throughout the novel she is tortured by her guilt in some
unnamed but readily apparent past relationship with one of
the British officers in the nearby fort. Always conscious of
her guilt, sometimes simply for its effect on her reputation,
more often for its effect on her inner character, she constantly seeks some way out of her past. But isolated on the
frontier, in touch only with a sister who in her feeble-minded
state of grace can neither understand nor genuinely sympa-
thize, and with a father—and eventually not even a real

father—who neither understands nor cares, Judith can turn only to the occasional men like Hurry Harry who are little better than her former lover. In its human depth such a situation constantly threatens to burst the decorous bonds of the sentimental novel. Given his audience of pure young maidens, Cooper was forced to present Judith only by indirection and by half-veiled hints. Given an audience that expected and demanded a tale of adventure on the frontier, Cooper was forced to subordinate her story to that of Indian fighting, "hair-breadth 'scapes i' th' imminent deadly breach or being taken by the insolent foe." Yet today Judith Hutter's character calls out in its human appeal over the shouting and confusion that surround her.

When Deerslayer appears in all his youth, strength, and incorruptible honesty, Judith's salvation seems at hand. His very innocence offers her mind a redemption from her own guilt. Yet the harder she tries to grasp it, the more elusively it slips away. For Deerslayer, blind to the human need that cannot be satisfied by the rifle or the "sarcumventions" of war, refuses her with cool ease. He has long known isolation but never real loneliness. Even at the moment in the story when he must meet his fate alone and singlehanded, he feels the ease of resignation and the comfort of pitting his solitary strength against the enemy. He feels the need for no outside human support and in any real sense wants none. When the greatest stress is over then, and he finds himself again the crafty woodsman free and alone in his beloved forest, it is no wonder that he feels no desire for the "community" of love. At the very beginning of the novel when Hurry Harry had been praising the yet unseen attractions of Judith, Deerslayer, aware of the rumors of her folly, had answered, " 'I would think no more of such a woman, but turn my mind altogether to the forest; *that* will never deceive you, being ordered and ruled by a hand that never wavers.' " [I, 23]

At the end of the novel he lives up to his promise, and it is one in keeping with his character and his thought revealed throughout the story. Thrown abruptly against such an unyielding and unflawed surface, Judith can only fall back stunned to her same unhappy predicament. The novel ends with her reported defeat—sufficiently ambiguous not to shock the young and modest—living with her former lover in England, without even the shallow satisfaction of a marriage.

The tragedy of Judith Hutter throws, then, an embarrassing light on the isolated uprightness of Deerslayer when his fidelity to the moral law is divorced from the obviously didactic purpose of the novel. For his law is supposed to be a sort of intuitive Christianity, natural to Deerslayer after the teachings of the Moravians. Yet it is an odd Christianity at best that does not include the principle of forgiveness; and Deerslayer offers little forgiveness. He carefully speaks against revenge—that is not the white man's "natur' "—but he continues to hold Judith's past follies against her despite her obvious repentance.

One of the most affecting moments of the novel comes at the end, when Judith, making one last desperate try, asks Deerslayer whether the rumors of her past are influencing his feelings toward her. He does not even reply, but she can read his answer in his countenance. One does not ask that he love her, but sympathy and understanding do not seem too great a moral commitment to expect. Deerslayer would be willing and even anxious to rescue her from savage Indians; he is unwilling even to attempt to rescue her from savage thoughts. And so Judith goes off as mortally wounded as those birds that Deerslayer so thoughtlessly shoots down. But Deerslayer the man of the forest comes to regret his killing of the helpless wildlife; the Deerslayer of the strict moral law apparently never regrets his wounding of a helpless human life.

To condemn Deerslayer for lacking spiritual sensitivity to the plight of others, however, is unfair to Cooper's intentions and would probably have shocked Cooper himself. For Deerslayer, in his crude good nature, his refined love for the forest life, his skilled knowledge of the forest frontier, is quite obviously meant to be the ideal woodsman—ideal almost in its literal sense—only human enough to catch the sympathy as well as the imagination of his audience. If he is not a perfect man, that, in a way, is as it should be; for *The Deerslayer*, despite its partially didactic purpose, is a novel, not about moral perfection or a saint on earth, not even about the perpetual human problem of moral commitment, but about the romantic dream of man on the American frontier escaping the need for commitment. Deerslayer is the fulfillment of the romantic myth of the frontiersman, the Daniel Boone of the northern woods; and, if anything, he is for the modern taste too good for his role, too much the dream and too little the real thing. The trouble is that the psychological character of Deerslayer, in comparison with the psychological character of Judith Hutter, raises the whole question of moral realism and will not let it be forgotten, and we would like to have him distinguished more clearly as either myth or reality. Perhaps it is simply the nature of myth, and its particular attraction, that makes such a distinction impossible: to divorce the myth from all reality would make it meaningless; to make it too real, too attached to the familiar world, would destroy the myth itself.

For Deerslayer to have understood Judith and to have offered something of himself to her would have been out of character for him, both in his way of thought and in his role in the novel. Similarly, for Judith to have found some source of human strength outside of herself would have been a glaring inconsistency in her role in the novel. For both are isolated beings on the lonely frontier. If she were alone by choice, the two could have been content in their mutual isolation. Or if he were alone only by the necessities of existence, they might have found a real community of love. But as they are, the possibility of any mutual relationship is unthinkable. One is lonely, but the other is not; and the two states of mind illustrate the two extremes of response to the isolation of the frontier. One embodies the romantic glory of the forest life, and the other the realistic sorrow; one the promise, and the other the threat. One illustrates the hopeful myth of the isolation of the frontier, the other the too common despairing reality. When Judith Hutter offers Deerslayer her father's rifle, the Killdeer that is to be his constant companion, she says, " 'Keep it, Deerslayer, and become King of the Woods.' " [II, 123–24] And he does keep it to become king of the woods with the only companion to whom he ever really gives his heart. Judith in turn can only go back to civilization, even all the way back to Europe, to try to escape her lonely existence.

The ideal world of the Deerslayer, then, is a far cry from the ideal world of Governor Bradford. In fact they are at opposite extremes: Bradford calls for greater sense of community and mutual responsibility, even as he sees his people begin to push out into the life of irresponsible individualism, the new lonely life of the frontier. Cooper calls for greater individualism, the romantic life of the lone hunter of the forest, even as he sees the city begin to grow and the lone hunter begin to disappear. As a logical element of the two ideals theirs are two opposite views of human isolation as well: the isolated life is to be avoided for spiritual as well as for practical reasons, or the isolated life is to be sought for spiritual as well as for practical reasons. Isolation is to be feared or to be favored.

The theme of human isolation as it appears in the American novel of the frontier would seem to have two possible but divergent paths to follow. Even at first glance, however, the choice is not quite so decisive as it might seem. One thought occurs immediately: Bradford is writing of real men on a real frontier facing real problems of isolation, but Cooper is writing of a romantic dream world, another part of the forest, where men are not forced to face the problems of real life. Romance is fine and enjoyable, but its theme may be somewhat different in conclusion from the theme of the novel trying to portray—or at least trying in a much more direct fashion to portray—the life that Americans must live. Then, too, the theme does not necessarily need to restrict itself to a consideration of just one of the two alternatives. By playing the romantic desire for Deerslayer's isolation against the moral demands of Bradford's the theme gains a complexity and an interest that are in keeping with the problem of isolation in real life. Cooper had the opportunity for just such a complexity when he introduced the character of Judith Hutter, but he let it slip away undeveloped and possibly even unnoticed.

Later novelists were not so blind to their opportunities or, perhaps rather, not so committed to the romantic ideal. Mark Twain's *Huckleberry Finn* provides a fine example. In his desire for romantic isolation, for the unhindered and uncommitted freedom of the forest, Cooper's Deerslayer speaks for the early frontier, or at least for the myth of the frontier. Twain's Huckleberry Finn at first wants the same uncommitted freedom, even though he does not speak so directly for the frontier as such. The Mississippi Valley through which Huck floats was admittedly not far removed from frontier conditions, and to a degree Huck represents these conditions, but for the most part he simply speaks for youth, whether it is the youth of a region or the youth of a man. He is the eternal longing of man to escape from the hindrances and the restrictions of social organization and social responsibility, the longing of man to live his own life for himself, following his will wherever it may take him.

His cry at the end of the novel is the cry for independence, whether it is the independence of the frontiersman or the vagabond: "But I reckon I got to light out for the Territory ahead of the rest, because Aunt Sally she's going to adopt me and sivilize me and I can't stand it. I been there before." [366] [2] This might almost be Deerslayer himself speaking, refusing any commitment to civilization, longing for the isolation of his forest. But of course it is not Deerslayer, who has a forest to live in alone, and for whom isolation is not a dream but a possible fact, or at least a fictional fact. It is a boy who against his will is constantly involved in the civilization that he would like to reject, but for whom there is no longer any real escape. If the Deerslayer is Huckleberry Finn grown older, Huckleberry Finn might be called the Deerslayer in an older country, put down in a time when the longing to escape is still a constant in youth, as always, but when the escape itself is rapidly becoming a thing of the nostalgic past. The Mississippi Southwest of the novel is passing from frontier to civilization, and Huck Finn is caught in the middle.

Just as his region is passing from youth to maturity, so is Huck Finn himself, and the novel is the story of his initiation to the problems of manhood. And a sure sign of his youth is his desire for the freedom that comes with isolation, for the rejection of the "sivilization" of man in society. Fortune has been kind to him here, hard as his lot is, for at the beginning of the novel at least he is almost wholly uncommitted. Family is no problem. The Widow Douglas and Miss Watson try their best, but an open window and a nearby shed always offer escape. When Pap does reappear, he is hardly one to

[2] Page references are to Mark Twain, *Adventures of Huckleberry Finn* (*Tom Sawyer's Comrade*) (New York: Charles L. Webster and Co., 1885).

civilize a boy. His own drunken hoggishness is, after all, only another form of escape from society, and one without the innocence or the harmlessness of youth. This is what happens when a man never grows up. Even when Pap forces Huck over the river to isolation in a deserted cabin, Huck enjoys the freedom of the life, smoking and fishing and cussing, with no books or manners to bother him. When Pap turns the cabin into a prison, Huck simply escapes and leaves it behind. For his only real parent he can feel neither love nor pity nor responsibility, and his foster parent is hardly a real one after all. The principal source of commitment for a boy, then, the family, does not even exist. And where it does, Pap is a source of isolation rather than a guard against it.

Friends and acquaintances are no better. Tom Sawyer is a friend, but outwardly at least he is in rebellion against civilization himself. It is, in fact, to Tom and his gang that Huck escapes from the family at night. But Huck cannot commit himself even in play to Tom and his romantic imagination. Somehow the gang of robbers is just a little silly, and Huck can see no profit in it: "I reckoned he believed in the A-rabs and the elephants, but as for me I think different. It had all the marks of a Sunday school." [33] Perhaps he even senses that in Tom's devotion to the romanticism of books there is a kind of commitment to civilization of just the sort he wants to escape. If everything has to be done by the book, there is no personal independence.

Later, on the river, the highway of freedom, there is no one except Jim to command allegiance. Even young Buck Grangerford, the son of feuding river aristocracy who might have become a real friend, belongs to a family that Huck cannot understand or feel any deep sympathy with. The feud in which Buck's family is engaged is enough to hold Huck at a distance, and the murder of Buck, much as it affects Huck emotionally, ends the possibility of friendship with complete finality. Huck is alone in life by instinct and by circumstance, and for a long time there is no one in his life to tempt him out of his isolation.

The river itself, like Deerslayer's forest, is Huck's only real friend, accepted and loved for what it is, always present as a source of companionship and solace and even protection. Again and again in the novel Huck returns to the river after some unpleasant experience on the banks, and it is like coming back to an old and trusted friend. There nothing can harm him, and nothing can restrain him except the river itself. Like any friend, the river, too, can have its moments of anger and of moodiness—it is never to be taken for granted—but Huck knows how to ride out the storm without loss of confidence or of faith. And in its moments of peaceful friend-liness the river can even lift a boy out of his loneliness:

When it was dark I set by my camp fire smoking, and feeling pretty satisfied; but by-and-by it got sort of lonesome, and so I went and set on the bank and listened to the currents washing along, and counted the stars and drift-logs and rafts that come down, and then went to bed; there ain't no better way to put in time when you are lonesome; you can't stay so, you soon get over it. [64]

Huck has a sympathetic understanding of the river that he never finds for any human, and he is willing to give himself to the river in a fashion that he never can to any human. But of course to say that the river is Huck's only real friend is only to say that Huck has no real friend, just as Deerslayer has none. In giving himself to the river he is in effect preserving that much more of the independence of his isolation.

Nigger Jim, Miss Watson's runaway slave, is the only human friend that Huck has on his trip down the river, the only person for whom he is willing to sacrifice something of himself. The finest part of the novel is, in fact, the growing friendship of the two. But Huck and Jim at first are so far apart that any real friendship seems impossible. Jim, after all, is an older Negro, and Huck a young white. The age perhaps makes little difference, for in many ways Huck has never really been young, and Jim, by the standards of civilization, has never really grown up. But the difference in color seems almost insurmountable, just as the difference in color does between Deerslayer and Chingachgook. Even when genuine friendship has miraculously sprung up, Huck never forgets Jim's color. Despite the desires of the modern sentimentalists, Huck remains a boy of the mid-nineteenth century South and does not lose his view of the Negro, even of Jim. His casual remarks are indicative; when he hears Jim mourning for his family he thinks, "I do believe he cared just as much for his people as white folks does for their'n." [201] And when Aunt Sally asks in concern about a steamboat explosion —one that Huck has made up for her benefit—whether any-one was hurt, he answers simply, " 'No'm. Killed a nigger.' " [280] Mark Twain's irony is apparent, but that does not change the character of Huck. Yet if Huck cannot see Jim as a man like himself, he can and does come to see Jim as a man and as a friend. The change is gradual, and it is only as a final achievement in the novel that Huck can accept Jim as a friend and free himself to surrender to him some portion of his protective isolation.

Perhaps as a result of his lonely state, or more likely as a concomitant, Huck carefully maintains the appearance at least of detachment from the world. At one point, when the King, one of the rascals who further Huck's feeling of aliena-tion from humanity, is planning one of his raids on the river bank, Huck says, "I see what *he* was up to; but I never said nothing, of course." [208] That "of course" is typical, for Huck seldom commits himself or even says what he is think-ing if he can help it. When he sees young Buck Grangerford

take an unprovoked shot at a Shepherdson he simply reports
the fact without comment. Or when he describes the loafers
in the Arkansas river town it is with a deliberately flat and
detached tone of voice: "There couldn't anything wake
them up all over, and make them happy all over, like a dog-
fight—unless it might be putting turpentine on a stray dog and
setting fire to him, or tying a tin pan to his tail and see him
run himself to death." [183] There is no censure, no sitting
in judgment, simply a statement of fact. This is perhaps the
blank and unself-conscious gaze of a young boy, but it has
also a quality of disillusionment, or rather lack of illusion.
Huck sees things for what they are, and wants no part of
them. But he will not commit himself even to being against
things; they go their way and he goes his, and he can remain
an isolated observer with his own thoughts.

By choice Huck remains detached, but by instinct he is
sympathetic, at least to decent people, and his sense of ethics
is deep even though hidden from the world. It is perfectly
clear what he thinks of the frauds of the King and the Duke,
for instance, and from time to time in telling the story he
even carelessly lets a remark escape: "It was enough to make
a body ashamed of the human race." [210] It is, in fact, this
instinctive morality that gives his detached gaze its real power
in the story; it implies an irony that is pervasive. Huck is
simply decent at heart, and he cannot hide the fact, try as he
will. Of course he is troubled by no petty considerations for
the institutionalized ethics of society. He is one of the world's
great liars—his ability to lie immediately and vividly and be-
lievably is one of the pleasures of the novel—and he does not
hesitate for a moment to let the end justify the means. (The
only time he completely fails is when he is lying for the King
and the Duke and cannot put his heart into it.) He can steal
in a small way without a second thought, although even then
he must sometimes rationalize his thefts to ease his conscience

a bit, as, for example, the time when he decides that it is all right to "borrow" fruit if he gives up crabapples—which he doesn't like much anyway—and persimmons—which won't be ripe for a few months. But when it comes to basic issues of human decency and sympathy there is no wavering and no hesitation. Huck cannot keep his feelings in isolation.

He is perpetually "in a sweat" over the predicament of someone else. At the circus—where he sneaked in, of course— he hears the crowd laughing at the drunk on a circus horse: "It warn't funny to me, though; I was all of a tremble to see his danger." [193] If it all turns out a joke, his sympathy is just as genuine. When it becomes obvious that the King and the Duke are going to rob the Wilks girls, Huck feels sorry for them and even determines to help them, for he responds immediately to the friendship and the decency that he has always found so rare. But his decency does not even require pity or a response to kindness; when Huck has trapped a couple of murderers on a steamboat about to go to pieces, he can even feel for them: "I begun to think how dreadful it was, even for murderers, to be in such a fix. I says to myself, there ain't no telling but I might come to be a murderer my- self, yet, and then how would *I* like it?" [103] Experience and circumstances have forced Huck into isolation from men, and he thoroughly enjoys the freedom that it brings, but, unlike Cooper's Deerslayer, that freedom does not mean for him a spiritual isolation. It becomes increasingly clear as the story goes along that he belongs to mankind by sympathy and by instinct, even though he would prefer to remain at a safe distance.

The central conflict of his isolation from mankind and his instinct toward sympathy is in his relationship with Jim. At first Jim is simply a companion, pleasant to have along on the raft to keep off loneliness but not someone to feel for or with in any real sense. To the end Jim is still a nigger to

Huck, but in a series of continuing shocks he becomes also a
man, and a man of dignity and decency and compassion.
Some of the shocks are the result of Huck's own thoughtless-
ness: Jim's pain at the rattlesnake bite for which Huck is
responsible and Jim's rebuke after Huck's practical joke on
the night of the fog. Some are the result simply of Jim's
humanity, as in his affecting story of slapping his deaf daughter, or of Jim's affection, as in the several times he welcomes
Huck back to the raft with such undisguised joy. Some are
the result of Huck's increasing awareness of Jim's unques-
tioning reliance on him. But most of all the companionship
just grows naturally between two likable and decent human
beings. And before Huck knows it he has begun to lose
something of his state of isolation; he has begun to give up
some of his unbounded freedom for the sake of another.
Huck does not change very much—the instinct toward compassion and friendship has always been there—but he is beginning to grow up. And growing up means surrendering some
of the self-centered desires of youth for some of the ethical
or altruistic necessities of true maturity. For Huck the voluntary surrender of complete isolation is the painful surrender of some part of his youth.

  Companionship and the resulting sense of responsibility
are not easy to give. They not only demand some loss of freedom and detachment, they also place Huck in an immediate
moral quandary. For with Jim's friendship he has also taken the
obligation to help Jim escape from slavery. But brought up,
insofar as he has been brought up at all, in a slave-holding
state, Huck believes that helping a slave escape is one of the
darkest crimes a boy can commit. It is a crime not only
against society in general but against the owner, Miss Watson, in particular, and Miss Watson has always been kind
to him. The quandary is a real one for Huck, and one not
to be resolved in an offhand fashion. It is only after agonized

self-appraisal and after several halfhearted attempts to give
Jim up that Huck finally arrives at that climactic moment in
the novel when he can tear up the letter that is to turn Jim
back to his owner and say, holding his breath, " 'All right,
then, I'll *go* to hell.' " [272] Huck is surprised, but the
reader is not, for he knows by now the power of Huck's
instinctive sympathy with the human lot, and he knows
the solidity of the friendship for Jim that has invaded Huck's
sense of isolation. From that moment Huck is no longer a
free and uncommitted boy but a youth who has taken the
first great moral step toward maturity, a step for which he has
been preparing himself all of his life, even though he did not
know it. The rest of the novel is anticlimax.

As Huck is turning the final decision over in his mind he
thinks first of the social duty that he has been taught: "It
would get all around, that Huck Finn helped a nigger to get
his freedom; and if I was to ever see anybody from that town
again, I'd be ready to get down and lick his boots for shame."
[269–70] This argument is not difficult for him to ignore,
for he feels so little responsibility to society anyway. Then
he begins to think of the problem in religious terms:

And at last, when it hit me all of a sudden that here was the plain
hand of Providence slapping me in the face and letting me know
my wickedness was being watched all the time from up there
in heaven . . . and now was showing me there's One that's
always on the lookout, and ain't agoing to allow no such miserable doings to go only so fur and no further, I most dropped in
my tracks I was so scared. [270]

This argument is more difficult to ignore and shows the
true heroism of his final decision: to choose deliberately to
go to hell for a friend is the highest sacrifice that love can
make. And Huck knows what hell is—Miss Watson had made
it all too clear.

Miss Watson's hell had apparently made an immediate impression on Huck, but the Widow Douglas's Christianity had made a deeper and a more lasting one:

She said the thing a body could get by praying for it was "spiritual gifts." This was too many for me, but she told me what she meant—I must help other people, and do everything I could for other people, and look out for them all the time, and never think about myself. This was including Miss Watson, as I took it. [29–30]

It is clear that in his decision to go to hell Huck is following the Widow Douglas's precepts but thinking of the problem in Miss Watson's terms, and the two seem to go in opposite directions. The result is a very real dilemma for Huck, despite the ironic simplicity it presents to the reader. The dilemma is particularly agonizing, for in a partial sense it echoes the dilemma in which Huck lives: the internal pressure toward isolation and freedom of the self, a way of life that pays off in the joy of uncommitted will, and the pressure toward sympathetic participation in the lot of others, a way of life that costs the voluntary loss of absolute freedom. But love of others wins over love of self, and the reader knows that despite Huck's despair heaven wins over hell.

It would be laughable to talk of Huck as if he consciously followed the Widow Douglas' teaching. In fact, immediately after she explains "spiritual gifts" to him, he decides the whole business is foolish: "I went out in the woods and turned it over in my mind a long time, but I couldn't see no advantage about it—except for the other people—so at last I reckoned I wouldn't worry about it any more, but just let it go." [30] Throughout the novel he remains skeptical about the benefits of religion, particularly organized religion, and has some wry observations to make about such things as the results of prayer and the habits of churchgoers:

There warn't anybody at the church, except maybe a hog or two, for there warn't any lock on the door, and hogs likes a puncheon floor in summer-time because it's cool. If you notice, most folks don't go to church only when they've got to; but a hog is different. [149]

Closer observation, however, shows that religious principles themselves are never mocked in the novel, only their misapplication. A case in point is Jim's story of giving ten cents to "Balum's Ass" because the preacher had said that whoever gave to the poor lent to the Lord and was bound to get his money back a hundred times. Sometimes in irony it is the church that is right, despite Huck's view and the congregation's blindness, as in the sermon preached to the feuding Grangerfords and Shepherdsons:

It was pretty ornery preaching—all about brotherly love, and such-like tiresomeness; but everybody said it was a good sermon, and they all talked it over going home, and had such a powerful lot to say about faith, and good works, and free grace, and preforeordestination, and I don't know what all, that it did seem to me to be one of the roughest Sundays I had run across yet. [148]

There is a lot of laughter in the novel about religious matters but never about religion. And what is equally interesting, the reader is never allowed to forget religious considerations for long. The constant joking keeps up the high spirits and the satiric flavor of the novel, but it also keeps up a thematic concern that is at the heart of the story.

While still thinking of the two sorts of Providence offered by Miss Watson and the Widow Douglas, Huck had come to a tentative conclusion about God: "I thought it all out, and reckoned I would belong to the widow's, if he wanted me, though I couldn't make out how he was agoing to be any better off then than what he was before, seeing I was so ignorant and so kind of low-down and ornery." [30] He soon forgets his conclusion, but at his decision to save Jim he finally brings it into climactic being. Without knowing it he has found a rational religious principle to match his irrational instinct. And the final decision is by no means simply instinctive. It is based on instinct or on natural impulse, of course, but that instinct had been matched against an equally strong instinct toward preservation of absolute freedom of self, and the decision followed only after careful thought.

It would be pleasant to note that the loss of self then leads to an even greater freedom, the great Christian principle, but this novel is not so rigorous or so final. If Huck Finn discovers the pleasures and the rewards of Christian charity, they are never recorded, or at least not in those terms. At best, and in a way it is a best, they are for him simply the pleasure and the reward that he finds in mankind getting along well together; "for what you want, above all things, on a raft, is for everybody to be satisfied, and feel right and kind towards the others." [166] The terms are those of a boy, but the feeling is in no conflict with Governor Bradford's demand for mutual concern growing out of spiritual charity.

The terms seem a little heavy, however, for Huck is, after all, only a boy drifting down the river, still clinging to the freedom of youth even though forced into the problems of maturity. He meets the problems, and he meets them in the right way, but he remains a boy, with all the freshness and spontaneity of boyhood. Perhaps it is right that the novel does not end before all the foolishness and the imaginative games at the Phelps farm. If it did, it would be entirely a novel of initiation into manhood; as it stands it is a novel of boyhood with the perennial appeal of boyhood to the adult mind. Perhaps the eventual source of dissatisfaction with the end of the novel is that Huck has just begun to leave boyhood behind, yet is at the end thrust back into it again. Nostalgia wins out over a potentially serious concern with human life. The novel is essentially an evocation of boyhood, and perhaps it is best that it refuses finally to leave that realm entirely. To the very end Huck is a representation of the absolute free will, the successful escape from "sivilization," that belongs to the realm of the desires and so is beyond the overly serious or solemn. His voluntary isolation, and to some extent even his involuntary, is part of a marvelous nostalgic dream world that haunts the American mind. The descriptions of the river life catch the whole mood:

A little smoke couldn't be noticed, now, so we would take some fish off of the lines, and cook up a hot breakfast. And afterwards we would watch the lonesomeness of the river, and kind of lazy along, and by-and-by lazy off to sleep. Wake up, by-and-by, and look to see what done it, and maybe see a steamboat, coughing along upstream, so far off towards the other side you couldn't tell nothing about her only whether she was stern-wheel or side-wheel; then for about an hour there wouldn't be nothing to hear nor nothing to see—just solid lonesomeness. [158]

To turn this evocation of a way of life that is apart from the harassment of the adult world to a solemn study of the spiritual problems of isolation would have been out of keeping with the novel as a whole. The human desire for the freedom of isolation is too strong to deny entirely.

The dream of Huckleberry Finn and the life of the drifting raft, then, is not so very different from the dream of the woodsman and the unrestricted freedom of the open forest. But it is a dream only, and the daytime life of the human being caught in a real world keeps intruding. Perhaps it is this combination that gives the novel its particular interest: it satisfies both the adult mind and the lingering mind of the boy. Bradford's conclusion and Cooper's dream meet in a momentary resolution that is both attractive and meaningful. The theme of human isolation in the novel of the frontier is

in process of transition from a concern with the romantic
desire of the myth of the frontier to the cold reality of
isolation in a real frontier world, and *Huckleberry Finn*
stands somewhere between, holding a fine precarious balance
that is like Huck Finn himself in balance between youth and
maturity or like the mid-nineteenth century Mississippi Valley
in balance between frontier and modern civilization. The
isolation of the raft is a wonderful freedom; as Huck says:
"Other places do seem so cramped up and smothery, but a
raft don't. You feel mighty free and easy and comfortable on
a raft." [156] But all along the banks the adult world is
waiting ready to spring. Sooner or later the shore can be
avoided no longer, and then isolation from mankind becomes,
not a joy and a freedom and an immunity, but a terror and
a spiritual restriction and a rejection of humanity. For a short
while in youth the American can move freely back and forth
from raft to shore, but when maturity demands a lasting answer the balance breaks down.

In the world of the American novel of the frontier that
maturity is well represented by Willa Cather's *My Ántonia*,
even though her novel like Twain's is largely concerned with
childhood. Even her setting is one that the adult mind
recognizes. Cooper's wilderness forest grew out of the myth
of the frontier and is a product of the romantic imagination
more than of the observant eye. It is the forest as it ought to
be, a forest that satisfies the romantic longings of its age. So,
too, with Natty Bumppo, the heroic king of the woods: a
character to capture the young imagination, to embody the
myth of the woodsman, but only occasionally to satisfy the
longing of mature man to recognize his kind. Some seventy-
five years later, in the frontier novel of Willa Cather one sees
a different wilderness and a different character. The frontier
has moved west to Nebraska, but in her fiction it has also
moved closer to the real experience of man. If her wilder-

ness and the people who live in it are sometimes idealized, at least it is an idealism that grows directly from experience. The romanticism that seems so fitting for Cooper's novel does not appear in Willa Cather's. Her frontier and her characters are occasionally softened and magnified by time, but time that does not distort noticeably and does not filter out the harsh and unpleasant. If her final effect approaches that of the myth, it is because she catches something of the timeless element of humanity in theme as well as in setting, not simply because she satisfies the romantic longings of a people and a time.

Cooper's forest and Willa Cather's farming frontier do have in common a concern with the isolation of the frontier, however sharply they may differ in the thematic conclusions they draw from the concern. In *My Ántonia* the new farmers of the Nebraska wilderness are isolated from one another and isolated from the past. So many, like the Shimerdas, have come directly from Europe and must suddenly face not only the rigors and the terrors of the wilderness but all the hostility and misunderstanding of the native for the foreigner. The Bohemians, the Danes, the Swedes, the Norwegians, the Russians, the Americans from the east coast must each live in a little isolated circle, mistrustful of the others and without aid or regard between groups. Many cannot even talk to others who do not speak the same language. And even for those who do, a common language does not always mean friendship. Peter Krajiek, the interpreter for the Shimerdas on their arrival, cheats them at every opportunity. In the early parts of *My Ántonia* only the narrator Jim Burden and his grandparents, a family with a sense of moral responsibility, can move with any ease from one national group to another, and then only at the cost of occasional misunderstanding and rebuff. Language, customs, inherent assumptions keep people apart as much as the wide-spreading prairie itself. Even the hostilities of the Old World are brought to the New, and the Bohemians and the Austrians keep up their old feud. On this raw middle frontier there is a distance of mind as well as a distance of space.

For the new frontier immigrant there is an added isolation too, for he is cut off, not only from his occasional neighbor, but more irrevocably from his distant homeland, the old country. There is no returning to the old, settled ways, the community and the tradition of the past, but only a future of lonely struggle in an alien land. For some, particularly for those untrained for the farming life, the struggle is too great. Mr. Shimerda, Ántonia's father, the gentle and amiable violinist, can end his homesick despair only by taking his own life. For others, the pioneer period can be endured until the new land becomes at last another homeland. Anton Cuzak, Ántonia's mild husband, had been apprenticed as a furrier in the old country, and his first years of frontier farming had been hard ones. But he had the mature Ántonia, a source of life and strength, to give him the love and the immediacy to pull him through.

And for those who do endure there is always hope for the children, the next generation, for whom the homeland is here about them, not impossibly beyond the seas. If the isolation of the prairies is one of homesickness and doubt, the future is still optimistic for those who come after. And the optimism is one that is sustained in *My Ántonia*, for the children of these first settlers, even though they may rapidly lose the pioneer virtues, do at least grow up within a new society in which they find their place. They need not be alone in the face of the wilderness, isolated from their past and from their fellow beings. It is no wonder that one of Mr. Shimerda's first requests to the Burdens is to teach Ántonia.

Yet even in the early days of this region which was just beginning to pass from wilderness to first complete settle-

ment the isolation is seldom absolute, for there is always the
family. The first explorers, the frontiersmen in the sense in
which Cooper had imagined them, had moved on in their
insatiable quest, and the farming families had arrived. The
Shimerdas and the Lingards, and for that matter the Burdens,
exist as more or less isolated groups, but groups nevertheless.
Perhaps until very recent days this has always been the situation of the farming region, here in the Nebraska wilds simply
intensified by the large region, small population, and the barriers of background and inheritance. In its very isolation the
family is forced into a sort of self-defensive unity; if there is
nowhere else to turn for aid and for companionship, the
family must turn within itself. To make his point of a complete frontier isolation Cooper was forced to destroy the
family unit, and the Hutters are neither in fact nor in feeling
a family. Certainly Huck Finn has no family at all, except for
a father who can hardly be called a father. Similarly Willa
Cather, to stress the early isolation of the Shimerdas, made
the family only an uneasy and unharmonious group, particularly in comparison with the Burdens or later with Ántonia
Cuzak's large family. Where there is no family love to offset
the isolation, existence is difficult for the sensitive individual
on the frontier, and Mr. Shimerda is destroyed by the loneliness as surely as Judith Hutter had been destroyed on another
frontier and in another time.

For Willa Cather human strength and endurance on the
frontier were in large part a matter of the strength of the
family unit. And as the pioneer days disappear in her novel
the family unity goes with them. The parallel to Bradford's
description of the disappearance of the communal unity at
Plymouth when the first frontier was conquered is striking;
Governor Bradford and Willa Cather are making the same
point. In *My Ántonia*, Jim Burden finds himself, almost
to his surprise, trying to hoodwink his grandparents once

he has settled down in the region. Many of the daughters of
the farming families begin to move into town as hired girls,
partly to make needed money for the family—family values
are not so easily lost—and partly to escape the isolation
and hard work of the farm. But many of the hired girls
never go home again and slowly drift away from Nebraska
entirely. They are no longer pioneers but simply young
American girls. The town itself, in fact, is a mark of the
disappearance of the early frontier—the Deerslayer hated
the towns for just that reason—and it is fitting that the
town of Black Hawk has importance only in the second half
of *My Antonia*. When the Burdens move into town, to be
followed by the country girls, it is a sign of what is happening
in the region. The high school, the ice cream parlor, Jelinek's
saloon, the dances at the Vannis pavilion and the Firemen's
hall, all are a denial of the isolation of the frontier and the
self-sufficiency of the family.

For all its huddling together and its social affairs, however, the town of Black Hawk is not so far from the isolation of the frontier as it might think. Jim Burden finds that
he can be as lonesome in town as on the farm and that the
national and social prejudices are as strong as ever. The immigrant farm girls are acceptable only as hired girls, and
the boys of eastern American stock will marry only their
own kind. Sylvester Lovett, the banker's son, may be in-
fatuated with the sensual Lena Lingard, but he solves his
problem by marrying an acceptable land-owning widow. The
town in all its petty isolation is best summed up by Jim
Burden during his discontented night prowls:

They were flimsy shelters, most of them poorly built of light
wood, with spindle porch-posts horribly mutilated by the turning lathe. Yet for all their frailness, how much jealousy and
envy and unhappiness some of them managed to contain! The life
that went on in them seemed to me made up of evasions and

negations; shifts to save cooking, to save washing and cleaning, devices to propitiate the tongue of gossip. This guarded mode of existence was like living under a tyranny. People's speech, their voices, their very glances, became furtive and repressed. Every individual taste, every natural appetite, was bridled by caution. [249-50] [3]

The farming frontier, for all its own loneliness, has at least its heroic struggle with the land and the seasons, its family pitted together against nature and all adversity.

The background of Ántonia Shimerda, then, is one of middle-frontier isolation. But she herself, like Jim Burden the narrator, is not lonely or unhappy. Just as the Deerslayer found self-fulfillment only in the isolation of the forest, and Huck Finn on the free-flowing river, so Ántonia finds self-fulfillment on the Nebraska prairie, although the fulfillment is of a quite different sort. Hers is neither the freedom of irresponsibility nor the romantic love of nature, the yearning for the primitive and unspoiled, the desire at heart for something distinct from the history and efforts of man, but rather love for the joining of man and nature into some greater whole than either can provide separately. The feeling is caught momentarily by Jim Burden on his arrival in Nebraska as he sits sunning himself in his grandmother's prairie garden:

I was something that lay under the sun and felt it, like the pumpkins, and I did not want to be anything more. I was entirely happy. Perhaps we feel like that when we die and become a part of something entire, whether it is sun and air, or goodness and knowledge. At any rate, that is happiness; to be dissolved into something complete and great. [20]

Coming early in the novel as it does, his feeling explains much of the mood of the novel and provides a preparation for

[3] Page references are to Willa Sibert Cather, *My Ántonia* (Boston and New York: Houghton Mifflin Co., [1918]).

what is to come and sympathy with the minds of the characters that Willa Cather likes.

Ántonia, paradoxically, is lonely only when she is caught up in the petty and artificial community life of the town: " 'I'd always be miserable in a city. I'd die of lonesomeness. I like to be where I know every stack and tree, and where all the ground is friendly. I want to live and die here.' "[362–63] On the prairie farm she expands to the limit of her being, and her inner horizon stretches toward the outer until the two join in one complete circle. Of course she is human and can have moments of loneliness: when her father dies she feels with him the isolation of her lot, and when she returns after being abandoned by her lover, feeling the momentary shame of her unborn child, she can only shrink within herself from the public gaze. But these moments pass and become in fact a part of her total feeling for life. She is no Coronado, whose memory is so carefully evoked, to die in the wilderness of a broken heart. And even in these moments of loneliness and depression she does not simply sit and suffer but throws herself with even greater vigor into the work of the farm. For work with the land is for her not simply a means of livelihood but a kind of immediate self-fulfillment. It is a means of joining her own being with that of nature and of drawing from each all of which it is capable, making of both one total being.

Jim Burden's final impression is one that catches up the essence of this organic unity:

She had only to stand in the orchard, to put her hand on a little crab tree and look up at the apples, to make you feel the goodness of planting and tending and harvesting at last. All the strong things of her heart came out in her body, that had been so tireless in serving generous emotions.

It was no wonder that her sons stood tall and straight. She was a rich mine of life, like the founders of early races. [398]

As Jim sees, there is something vital about Ántonia that springs from the solitary land and returns to it again, making the land something more than just land. On the first arrival of the farming pioneers there had been nothing but grass and space: "There was nothing but land: not a country at all, but the material out of which countries are made." [8] But years later, at the height of Ántonia's vitality, there are land and life and love—a family and a farm that defeat the isolation of the frontier and make human life and prairie nature one unified condition that can be called a country. The large family and the fruitful farm are the products of Ántonia, the "rich mine of life," but they are only outward and visible signs of an inward and even spiritual grace. For Ántonia is herself the spirit of the whole man and the prairie, the one unified being who can, not transcend the isolation and loneliness of the wilderness, but rather make of that isolation something fruitful and satisfying and complete.

For Willa Cather such a spirit is the real answer to the isolation of the American frontier. There are other answers, but none is so complete and so satisfying. The easiest, of course, if it is an answer at all, is simply to leave the farm as soon as possible. This is the answer of Lena Lingard, the literary foil to Ántonia in the novel, and for her at least it is not a contemptible answer either. By nature Lena does not belong on the frontier. With her sensual attraction and her pleasure-loving nature she is a girl of artificial civilization. It is fitting that she becomes a dressmaker, and a successful one, for the very luxury and artificiality of the craft is in keeping with her nature. The family to Lena is not a source of strength and vitality but rather a clog for her own development and a source of irritation and hindrance. Like Ántonia, she is not afraid of loneliness, but, unlike Ántonia, she wants a loneliness only of the sort that leaves her free and unhindered. When Jim Burden tells her that she will soon tire of the life in Lincoln and will want a family, she answers:

"Not me. I like to be lonesome. When I went to work for Mrs. Thomas I was nineteen years old, and I had never slept a night in my life when there weren't three in the bed. I never had a minute to myself except when I was off with the cattle." [329]

And Lena never does marry, despite her immediate attraction for men. She retains her inner isolation to the end, unwilling to merge it with the isolation of the land to become, by the paradox lived by Ántonia, "a part of something entire."

The Ántonias of the frontier, however, are rare. If they were not, the character would not be unique, as it is in this novel. Yet this Ántonia does represent something of the abiding human value of the isolation of the middle frontier, if only as a sort of ideal or potentiality. And Willa Cather, in other novels as well as this one, recognizes all too clearly that it is an ideal rapidly being lost: *O Pioneers!*, *The Song of the Lark*, *A Lost Lady*, *The Professor's House*, *Death Comes for the Archbishop*, *Shadows on the Rock*, all touch at least on the loss of a frontier ideal. But *My Ántonia* seems to place Willa Cather's sense of loss most clearly and most poignantly. In a somewhat fanciful sense, she herself is the most isolated and most lonely character of the novel. Jim Burden, the fictional narrator, after marrying a woman entirely unlike Ántonia comes back to Nebraska for a visit, and he says, "I had the sense of coming home to myself." [419] In this mood he speaks for the entire novel. His recognition of the spiritual achievement of Ántonia, the deeper value of her character as it merges with that of the fruitful prairie, is a recognition of what he has himself missed, although he does not put the feeling in so many words. For he has refused the Nebraska life—although he has never rejected it— and feels the resulting loss. Rather ironically he has kept a

slender tie by becoming legal counsel for one of the great
Western railways. Without trying to draw any close parallel,
the general analogy to the biography of Willa Cather herself
is there by clear implication. Perhaps the general analogy
would even help to explain the somewhat unsatisfactory
character of Jim, who is a man but so often in the novel
does not think or respond as a man would. Willa Cather
has put so much of herself into him that she to some extent
loses control of him as a fictional character.

Whatever the biographical analogy, the novel itself has a
clear mood of loneliness to convey to the reader. The words
"lonely" and "loneliness" appear often in the novel, but the
key word, occurring with enough frequency to make it a
sort of verbal leitmotiv, is "homesick." Examples are ever
present: "I knew it was homesickness that had killed Mr.
Shimerda." [115]; "For the first time it occurred to me
that I would be homesick for that river after I left it." [266];
" 'It makes me homesick, Jimmy, this flower, this smell,' she
said softly." [269]; " 'It seems like my mother ain't been
so homesick, ever since father's raised rye flour for her.' "
[272] The word is right and proper, for this is a homesick
novel. The pioneer families look back to the old country
left behind and are homesick. Their children look back to
the days of their childhood and are homesick. The novel
itself looks back to the days of the middle frontier and is
homesick. Only Ántonia resists this form of loneliness, for
where she is she makes a home. But she in turn provides a
source of homesickness, for she is the ideal of the frontier,
a spirit to be looked back upon with longing from the present
state of loneliness, a being complete in a world now incomplete.

My Ántonia is a novel about the past. Cooper had set The
Deerslayer a century back in time, Twain had set Huckleberry Finn back nearly half a century, and Willa Cather sets

the principal part of her novel back some thirty years or more. For all three, whatever their different views of human isolation and their different thematic answers to it, the frontier had disappeared and now belonged to a more heroic time in the past. Willa Cather's past has a particularly nostalgic tint, for it leads to the homesickness of the present. And the nostalgia in turn gives the past a suggestive value, leading, in one sense, to a softness of outline but, in another, to a vividness of impression that makes the moment or the object almost clearer and sharper than life itself. The momentary vision in the novel of the silhouette of a plow against the setting sun, a familiar example of the art of Willa Cather, stands as an example. It is almost too sharp, too perfect, yet it has a high suggestive value that captures the imagination. So, too, the events of Jim Burden's childhood—or Willa Cather's past—stand out in sharp and simplified outline, suggesting a time of heroic dimensions now gone. To this past the novel comes home again from a lonely and isolated present. "Some memories are realities, and are better than anything that can ever happen to one again." [370] To those without the character of an Ántonia, the mature strength to see the self in relationship—almost moral relationship—to the surrounding world, isolation can be an element of time as well as of space, and loneliness is not restricted to the old frontier.

At this point the conclusion that *Huckleberry Finn* had suggested in the theme of isolation, the moral necessity for isolation to see itself in the perspective of the rest of humanity if it is to avoid the pain of loneliness, comes to its fulfillment. *My Ántonia* is thematically a long way from *The Deerslayer*, even if *Huckleberry Finn* is considered a step along that way. If isolation is not necessarily to be avoided, it is certainly not to be sought; and the most admirable is not the one who turns away from other humans and from ordinary life but the one who turns toward them for completeness of spirit. The answer that Bradford had urged for the question of isolation has proved the enduring one even though the literal frontier has disappeared in America. We still have our Huck Finns and our Ántonias—and for that matter our Natty Bumppos too—even though their backgrounds and their settings have gone. The frontier in America, and in its novel, has become a matter of mind or of view rather than a matter of place. But the problem of human isolation, made so vivid and immediate by the old frontier, remains a constant in American life on its new frontiers and continues to find its theme in the American novel.

The new frontier, however, may take curious forms. If *Huckleberry Finn* is a nostalgic evocation of boyhood on the middle frontier, free and uncommitted, drifting along through a dirty world but untouched by it, J. D. Salinger's *The Catcher in the Rye* seems almost a travesty of the earlier novel. As young Holden Caulfield runs away from the preparatory school that he is being expelled from anyway, and spends three lost days drifting through New York City before surrendering to home and family, he inevitably suggests Huck Finn's running away from "sivilizing," only to be caught again at last. But a hundred years in time have passed, and the frontier of the Mississippi Valley, like Deerslayer's forest a hundred years before that and Willa Cather's Nebraska of a later day, has turned into the modern frontier of New York City, where there is always the chance to begin life again in lonely isolation in the midst of the seven million people, but where freedom is only a lost dream and a desperate desire of the modern Huckleberry Finn. There is no river of escape here, no deep and dark forest, no endless prairie, only a grimy hotel room and a dark and threatening Central Park.

Huck Finn and Holden Caulfield have much in common. Both are essentially decent, and both boys judge the world by an inner standard of respect for the dignity and well-being of others. Just as Huck is constantly in a sweat over the predicament of someone else, so Holden worries about others and hates those who would hurt them. Even Ackley, the "nasty guy" in the next room at Pencey Prep, can arouse sympathy as well as irritation in Holden. The thought of a former schoolmate tortured by his fellows until he jumps out of the window can sicken him. Both boys are running away from the imprisonment of their civilized world to seek the life of uncommitted freedom, and both are committed by their very moral nature to the human being that constitutes their imprisonment. Even Huck cannot escape entirely, for there is always the decision to be made about Jim. But Holden cannot escape at all, for his world of New York turns out to be really no different from the world of Pencey Prep. But both try to escape, and the effort itself places them in the same world of boyhood at that stage in which the boy is being forced inevitably into the dirty world of manhood—or at least of men. And the moment of transition is the story as well as the character of both, unlike the story of Deerslayer in his imaginary world of the past that allows a perpetual youth in a perpetual world of freedom.

Yet Holden Caulfield is different in many ways from Huck Finn despite their common ties. For one thing, he is neither so innocent nor so disillusioned. Huck seems to have been born with the detached gaze of one who can no longer be shocked by the actions of men. Occasionally something particularly gross will bring out a comment on the damned human race, but in general he maintains his almost disinterested view of even the most shocking occurrences. At the same time, he seldom seems to suspect the worst and is caught by surprise when it arrives. Holden, on the other hand, not only suspects the worst, he expects it. And he is loud—at least with his inner voice—in condemning the world as he finds it, never settling down to a stoical acceptance of things as they are. His language of bright adolescence seems particularly fitted to his constant outrage: the world is full of "slobs" and "phonies" and "mean guys" and "big deals" who leave him always "depressed." He knows that the world of school and the world of the city are full of repulsive people, and he is sure that even if he could escape these worlds, he would find the same people anywhere else. Even the ultimate escape of a monastery would be just the same thing over again: " 'The kind of luck I have, I'd probably join one with all the wrong kind of monks in it. All stupid bastards. Or just bastards.' " [65] [4]

The difference in view and in emotional response of the two boys is the difference too in the problem of isolation in the two novels. Huck simply wants to be allowed to enjoy his own pursuits. He has nothing against mankind and is perfectly willing to join the race whenever he feels the desire. Holden is caught in a more complex emotional state springing from the more complex world in which he lives, and it is no wonder that he writes his story while apparently recovering from a mental breakdown. For he wants to escape the society he knows and at the same time wants to be a part of the more nearly perfect society that he can imagine—not that he ever imagines it directly, although he is at least keenly aware that it does not exist now. Caught between two impossibilities, he can only fall back on an isolated scorn, an adolescent rage colored by a moving, even a pathetic, longing for loss of isolation among the honest and the true and the decent human beings who ought to exist—who must exist—in greater numbers somewhere.

All he knows at the moment is that as he looks about him he sees only a world of "phonies," of sham and pretense,

[4] Page references are to J. D. Salinger, *The Catcher in the Rye* (Boston: Little, Brown & Co., 1951).

or a world so devoted to selfish exclusiveness or shallow
pleasures or degrading self-contentment, if not to more
active cruelty, that a boy with self-respect and common
decency and some feeling for the potentialities of the human
being cannot be a part of it. His fellow students, like Stradlater and Ackley, are self-contented "slobs." Most of his
teachers are "phonies," like the headmaster who ignored the
unfashionable parents for those who wore the right clothes;
and the few that are not "phonies," like old Spencer, the
history teacher, never really understand him and are likely to
be bores anyway. New York is full of pimping and crooked
bellboys, tourists looking for celebrities, conceited intel-
lectuals, Ivy League types, brainless girls who only want to
say and do the proper fashionable things. Even looking ahead
to the standard professional life that he fears is before him,
he sees nothing there to attract: " 'All you do is make a lot
of dough and play golf and play bridge and buy cars and drink
Martinis and look like a hot-shot.' " [223] It is enough to
make anyone depressed. Part of the fascination of this novel
is Holden's angry criticism of our civilization; an adolescent
prophet, but a prophet none the less.

One way out would be literal isolation. New York cannot
offer it, so he will run away with old Sally to Vermont and
chop his own wood. The dream of Deerslayer in the forest
is not yet dead. But old Sally is entirely too proper a girl
even to think of such a thing. Or better, he could go west—
again the old frontier—and lead a life of complete isolation
as a deaf-mute:

That way I wouldn't have to have any goddam stupid useless
conversations with anybody. If anybody wanted to tell me something, they'd have to write it on a piece of paper and shove it
over to me. They'd get bored as hell doing that after a while,
and then I'd be through with having conversations for the rest
of my life. Everybody'd think I was just a poor deaf-mute

bastard and they'd leave me alone. They'd let me put gas and oil in their stupid cars, and they'd pay me a salary and all for it, and I'd build me a little cabin somewhere with the dough I made and live there for the rest of my life. I'd build it right near the woods, but not right *in* them, because I'd want it to be sunny as hell all the time. [257–58]

Although the forest is gone now, and Holden knows it, he almost starts hitchhiking west. Salinger is almost too heavily ironic when Holden finally ends in the care of a psycho-analyst in a kind of rest home in the Far West.

It is typical of Holden, however, that even in his cabin in the woods he makes room for a wife, just as he wants to take old Sally to Vermont with him. His red hunting hat may suggest Deerslayer and the solitary hunter, but, like Deerslayer, he wants some kind of companion at least. Companionship does not mean groups of people, for groups always seem organized on the wrong principle. The other boys at school would hang around together simply because they had something in common, no matter what. " 'Even the guys that belong to the goddam Book-of-the-*Month* Club stick to-gether.' " [170] In fact, groups are part of the very atmos-phere that he is trying to escape. At school the clannishness had seemed its worst. The very worst thing there was the fraternity that Holden says he was too "yellow" not to join. His whole scorn and hatred for the school had come to a focus on the refusal of the fraternity to take in a boy, Robert Ackley, whom Holden did not like but who had nothing much wrong with him beyond unpopularity: " 'Just because he was boring and pimply. I don't even feel like talking about it. It was a stinking school. Take my word.' " [217–18] It is clear that Holden is not himself an unpopular boy; his isola-tion is of his own choosing. But he cannot accept his fellows in social groups, human nature being what it is.

With no escape open from the worst of "civilization," and

with no desire for a life of complete isolation—however tempting it may look at a distance—as well as no real possibility
of achieving it, Holden is left in his dilemma: he is isolated
from the human being, yet in the midst of human beings; he
longs for isolation, yet wants to avoid loneliness; he runs
away from "civilization," yet finds himself securely engulfed
in it. The only way out is the way he finds, or at least begins
to find, at the end of the novel. He will continue to be the
isolated individual in the teeming modern world, giving up
even the dream of the impossible escape to the forest, and
will gradually discover an affection for those other individuals who show some potentiality at least of decency
and the ability to like and to be liked. The conclusion is
hardly startling, but it is one he reaches only through the
long isolated search that is the story of *The Catcher in the
Rye*.

Holden has always had the beginning of his answer, perhaps even one part of it, for, despite his view of the damned
human race, he has always been able to recognize whatever
is likable or admirable even in those he dislikes. Stradlater is
a "secret slob," a conceited girl chaser, but Holden notices
that he would give you the tie from around his neck. Or
there is Harris Macklin, a former roommate: "He never
stopped talking, and what was awful was, he never said anything you wanted to hear in the first place. But he could do
one thing. The sonuvabitch could whistle better than anybody I ever heard." [161] He refuses to classify anyone as
wholly boring or repulsive—maybe he is secretly a terrific
whistler too—and the result is a refusal to cut himself off
from any chance of a meaningful relationship to the other
individual.

The trouble is that, in addition to the difficulty of discovering the unsuspected generosity or the talent for whis-
tling, Holden finds it almost impossible to discover a means

of communication with others, a meeting of mind and will
that could deny the isolation in which he lives with his own
thoughts and desires unknown to others. When he goes in
to see old Spencer, the teacher who takes a genuine interest
in him, he knows that Spencer is trying to be kind and
helpful, but he also knows that the two will never really
understand each other—they are just "too much on opposite
sides of the pole, that's all." [20] He would like to tell the
one man who shows him any kindness why he has done so
badly at school, but he knows there is no point: "He wouldn't
have understood it anyway." [18]

Between teacher and student or between old and young
the situation may be normal, but that does not help Holden's
sense of isolation any. And the lack of understanding is not
restricted to his relations with adults. Even old Sally, the
proper young thing that he dates in New York in an attempt
to find someone to save him from his loneliness, never
understands quite what he is talking about, and certainly
never what he is thinking. When he impetuously asks her
to run away with him she holds before him instead the
proper pattern of a proper life for a proper young girl.
Holden tries to explain the difference but can finally say
only, " 'You don't see what I mean at all.' " [173] The next
moment he is angry and insulting, the only course that
seems open to him, since it is better to be completely apart
than half together.

The one line of communication for Holden, the one way
of establishing contact with others, is that of affection.
And Holden is always quick to offer affection as well as to
respond to it. He is even prepared to like the stupid, pathetic
girls he picks up in the hotel club room if they would only
give him the chance. Or again, he goes out of his way to
like Mrs. Morrow, the mother that he meets on the train,
and to make her happy tells her that her son, "the biggest

bastard that ever went to Pencey, in the whole crumby history of the school," [71] is a fine, popular boy. He likes her, partly because of his affectionate nature and partly in response to her apparent liking for him expressed without condescension. For Holden is sensitive to affection and needs it as any isolated, unhappy child does.

Paradoxically and a little pathetically, it can even make him "depressed" when he finds evidence of affection, for he is not really used to it and feels that somehow he is letting down the other person. Even the failure to use the skates his mother had sent as a present can leave him downcast: she had sent him the wrong kind of skates, but still he was failing her trust by being expelled again. And her present just made things worse. "Almost every time somebody gives me a present, it ends up making me sad." [67] With such a nature and such a need, and with his ability to suspect, if not to find, something likable in any person, he cannot be depressed by the state of mankind and the pain of isolation for the rest of his life. He only needs someone to point the way out, to show him how to escape from the shell of his isolation without escaping from humanity itself.

The someone is his young sister Phoebe. There are others who might have filled the role but did not. Old Jane, the girl he is half in love with, may be as fine as he imagines her, but Holden somehow never quite gets around to talking to her in the course of the novel. The reader wonders why. The family that Antonia found so important hardly exists for Holden. His parents and his older brother are little more than shadows in the novel, sensed only vaguely and at a distance. He has apparently no very close relationship with his mother, and his father represents the archetype of the successful lawyer of which Holden is so contemptuous. The echo of Huck Finn is heard once again. His older brother, D. B., of whose writing Holden was once so proud, has let him down: he is out in Hollywood writing trash for the movies. His younger brother, Allie, who died a few years before the time of the novel, is a remembered object of affection (in part tinged for Holden with a familiar sense of guilt for his boyish neglect) but one that makes Holden's situation worse, since he can meet him now only in imagination divorced from the living. Only Phoebe remains, and she is more than adequate for the role.

The scene in which Holden sneaks into the family apartment at night to see Phoebe is not only one of the most affecting scenes of the novel—Phoebe is one of the genuinely attractive children in literature—but one of the most important. Here for the first time Holden finds immediate warmth and love:

"Holden!" she said right away. She put her arms around my neck and all. She's very affectionate. I mean she's quite affectionate, for a child. Sometimes she's even *too* affectionate. I sort of gave her a kiss, and she said, "Whenja get *home?*" She was glad as hell to see me. You could tell. [209]

And, almost as important to him, he finds immediate understanding. He tells her of what has happened to him and why he hates a school full of phonies and mean guys. For the first time someone really listens to him: "She always listens when you tell her something. And the funny part is she knows, half the time, what the hell you're talking about. She really does." [218] It is here—fittingly—that he tells her the half-dream that explains the title of the novel: he would like to be the "catcher in the rye" that keeps little children from falling over a cliff. The unconscious symbolism is obvious—childhood and innocence and likability, and the cliff waiting at the edge—and helps to explain the elements of Holden's mind that make him a lonely, isolated boy but one capable of salvation. When he finally sneaks out of the

apartment again—ironically, at the return of his parents—
Phoebe presses on him her Christmas money, and the
gesture of love and generosity is too much for him. For
the first time in the novel he cries, and the tears are the
beginning of the loss of the stoic pride and bitterness that
have been sustaining his isolation.

The end of the novel, when Phoebe tries to insist on going
west with Holden, is almost a continuation of the same
scene. She meets him at the Museum, that one spot of stability
in a changing world, although even that dirtied by man's
writing on the wall, dragging along an old suitcase to ac-
company him wherever he wants to go. In her own child's
way she will not take his "no" for an answer. The gesture
of love is too much for him, and the novel ends with Holden
sitting in the rain—the traditional suggestion of rebirth—
watching her go around on the carrousel: "I felt so damn
happy all of a sudden, the way old Phoebe kept going around
and around. I was damn near bawling, I felt so damn happy,
if you want to know the truth. I don't know why." [275]
But the reader knows why. Holden has begun to break out
of the shell of his isolation; or, perhaps better, the shell has
been cracked by Phoebe, aided by his almost unconscious
efforts from within.

There is no astonishing and immediate transformation, of
course, for it will presumably be years before he can take
his full place in life. In the little coda to the novel, added as
Chapter 26, he writes that despite the psychoanalyst he
does not himself know whether he will go back to school
that year and "apply himself." But he does know that he
now wants to see again those acquaintances who at least
are human and some of whom might even be friends: "About
all I know is, I sort of *miss* everybody I told about. Even old
Stradlater and Ackley, for instance." [277] He had said
before that he never really hated anybody for long, and

began to miss them after a while, but now even the hatred begins to give way before the idea of love and affection in the world. If he is lonesome now, it is just because of the absence of friends, not because of the presence of too many contemptible people. After all, there is affection in life, there is even love for some, and the world may well be full of secret whistlers.

The world of the old frontier is gone, and with it the Huck Finns and the Deerslayers who can happily follow their own free natures. The Deerslayers particularly belong to a time long dead: a time when a man could be happy alone in the woods and maintain his self-respect by simply ignoring the needs and the natures of the other humans whom he meets. Isolation for Deerslayer was a state to be sought, and others either did not exist in this state or, perhaps better, ought not to exist. But one suspects that such a man and such a state never were; Deerslayer is the romantic dream of escape, of perpetual youth with no need and no demand for moral commitment. Huck Finn, the real youth, comes closer to human nature—and closer to Holden Caulfield—in his commitment. He may run, like a young Daniel Boone, from civilization to a free isolation, but he never cuts himself off from humanity. In many ways he is even kin to young Ántonia Shimerda. She is isolated on the prairie involuntarily —unlike Huck and the Deerslayer, who deliberately seek their isolation—but she finds that commitment to life, to others, is the final need of her nature, the answer to the isolation that might be, for her at least, so frightening. She still has somewhere to run, if she wanted to run and if she had a plaguing civilization to run from. But, like Holden, she finds that running cannot solve her problem. Isolation, like the frontier itself, is a matter of mind rather than of circumstance.

Holden Caulfield, then, serves as a modern review of these

other novels of the American frontier. He dreams of the uncommitted isolation of a Deerslayer and, like Huck, runs away from the one form of "civilization" he knows best. But there is nowhere to run to any more, and he finds that, like Ántonia or, to a lesser extent, like Huck Finn, he must live with his own isolation and defeat it on its own terms. The victory that he finally wins, the answer that he discovers for himself through the love of old Phoebe, is the answer that Bradford on his frontier had given Americans three hundred years before: a man cannot live within himself in contempt of the world; he must be a part of that human race to which he is by nature morally committed; a decent regard, even a potential love for others, is the unavoidable requirement for life in America—or anywhere else—if a man is to avoid the torture of isolation that American life can bring. This is both the problem of the isolation of the frontier and its answer, the answer that Cooper at his safe romantic distance never suspected. And this is one reason why Twain and Willa Cather and Salinger are more satisfying than Cooper to real Americans who must live on their own real frontiers.

III

The Mighty Individual

Thomas Wolfe's *Look Homeward, Angel* is a direct exploitation of the American sense of isolation, in the tradition perhaps of the frontier novel, although not concerned with the frontier. It is a novel about young Eugene Gant, the lonely boy growing up in a lonely land and, by clear extension, about all the lonely young Americans. Wolfe spares no words in establishing Eugene as the representative, though hardly typical, American boy. From the introductory prose verse—"Which of us has known his brother? Which of us has looked into his father's heart? Which of us has not remained forever prison-pent? Which of us is not forever a stranger and alone?" [2] [1]—through the bulk of the story itself—"And the old hunger returned—the terrible and obscure hunger that haunts and hurts Americans, and that makes us exiles at home and strangers wherever we go" [423–24]—the novel is meant to speak for the American, or at least for the young American. Thomas Wolfe denies that Eugene is entirely an autobiographical character, and with good reason, for the character was to be all the young Thomas Wolfes crying out against the isolation from other humans that Wolfe felt within himself.

And Thomas Wolfe succeeded. Today *Look Homeward, Angel* is usually first discovered by the young who take it to heart as an expression of the loneliness that they cannot

[1] Page references are to Thomas Wolfe, *Look Homeward, Angel; A Story of the Buried Life* (New York: Charles Scribner's Sons, 1929).

express for themselves. They are meeting the problem that Wolfe meets, not only the problem of the isolation itself, the feeling of exile from family as from strangers, but the closely related problem of lack of understanding between fellows that is both the cause and the effect of the isolation. Even that imaginary (and amusingly improbable) baby of the Gants looks out from his crib, unable to communicate with others, seeing their inability to communicate with each other:

He saw that the great figures that came and went about him . . . had for one another not much greater understanding than they had for him: that even their speech, their entire fluidity and ease of movement were but meagre communicants of their thought or feeling, and served often not to promote understanding, but to deepen and widen strife, bitterness, and prejudice. [38]

Eugene's feelings and perceptions are no different as he grows older. His father had found the same experience: "He saw more clearly than ever that he was a stranger in a strange land among people who would always be alien to him" [22]; and now young Eugene must go through the discovery for himself. Perhaps, like so much in his character, he has inherited the feeling from his family. His father with his halfhearted attempt to find some form of escape and communication in the art represented by his tombstone carving might be the first source. But his mother, lost in her irresistible itch for possession of property, contributes her share too. And then the other children of the family intensify the atmosphere of isolated existence: Luke with his jeering sense of detachment; Helen with her possessive instinct that would share with no one else a place in the heart; most of all Ben, the sensitive, lost outcast from the family. Young Eugene is a Gant through and through, born and bred a member of a family at the opposite extreme from the close-knit group of an Ántonia Shimerda, and he can never escape the emotions of his family.

So *Look Homeward, Angel* is one long cry of hurt and outrage at the lonely state of the young American who feels the unbridgeable chasm between his own inner life and the lives of the fellow humans about him. Like the man who cannot leave the aching toe alone, Eugene Gant even seeks the isolation that pains him. After the first shock of rejection and humiliation at the university, "Pulpit Hill," he seeks "a physical isolation, hard enough to bear at first, which later became indispensable to him, mind and body." [403] Then, paradoxically, the method succeeds in gaining easy acceptance for him from fellow students. For the first time he is happy, or at least believes he is: "He was happier than he had ever been in his life, and more careless. His physical loneliness was more complete and more delightful." [487–88] And so his life is set, a decision to be followed in this novel by an angry denunciation and rejection of the family, a series of lonely wartime jobs around Norfolk and Newport News, and finally the vision of the life before him: "To go alone, as he had gone, into strange cities; to meet strange people and to pass again before they could know him; to wander, like his own legend, across the earth—it seemed to him there could be no better thing than that." [527] The angry fear of isolation becomes a tortured acceptance of it as the only satisfactory lot of man, and Eugene is to go on alternately self-pitying and self-congratulatory, never satisfied, never finding the home of his own lost soul, never ceasing the search.

At the end of *Look Homeward, Angel* he thinks he has found an answer. " '*You* are your world,' " [624] the ghost of his brother Ben tells him, and Eugene knows that his only future, his only real being, is within himself:

He stood naked and alone in darkness, far from the lost world of the streets and faces; he stood upon the ramparts of his soul, before the lost land of himself; heard inland murmurs of lost seas, the far interior music of the horns. The last voyage, the longest, the best. [625]

His future is to be within, isolated from others, struggling to communicate his own inner thoughts to those without. He is to be self-existent, self-contained, self-replete. He is to be man but not of men, a member of mankind but not of the society of men. His covenant is not with others but with himself.

Perhaps that is what is wrong with *Look Homeward, Angel*. " 'I'm a stranger in a strange land,' " Eugene's father had once said to his mother. And she had answered—to the later scorn of Eugene—" 'Pshaw! You ought to get out and meet more people. You need something to take your mind off yourself.' " [11] The reader today, after the first youthful enthusiasm, is tempted to make the same answer to Eugene, whatever the scorn he might expect from the ghost of Thomas Wolfe. For the continual self-pity of the novel, the self-indulgent rhetoric, the constant exploration of an unhappy but confused and undecided mind, begins to lose its interest before the novel is done. One wants some greater intelligence, some maturity of mind, brought to the picture of youth and adolescence; one wants, for final satisfaction, to know that there is in the world a maturity to be sought at last, whatever the mind of youth may be. One wants, in short, something more than the mind of Eugene Gant, some hint at least that there is a world of man without as well as within.

Whatever dissatisfaction the novel may arouse, however, it does touch firmly, without indirection—even without sub-tlety—on the problem of human isolation in America that has fascinated the American author from the beginning of the nation. Thomas Wolfe in the twentieth century, as had William Bradford in the seventeenth, has defined the problem and shown its immediacy for life in America. Both men's books are histories in their own way: Wolfe's an autobiography, often exaggerated and sometimes made up from his own imagination where necessary to stress the points that he felt important and representative in his experience; Bradford's an account of the first Puritan experience in America, as factually accurate as he could make it, but so sweeping and yet so detailed, so climactic in movement, as almost to give the impression of fiction. And both in a way, like so many American novels, concern youth: the youth of a country and the youth of an individual; a time of turmoil and experiment and discovery for a young country and a young man, held apart from others, groping for some satisfactory answer to an isolation that is simultaneously a torment and an attraction.

The differences, of course, are greater than the similarities, if for no other reason than the difference in the two authors. Bradford is mature, reflective, confident of the truth; a disappointed man at the end of his story but able to control his disappointment by an ultimate confidence in God's will. Wolfe is young, tormented, impulsive, wildly searching for some truth to which he can hold; apparently full of self-pity and narcissistic indulgence for his failure to find all the answers. But an even greater difference is apparent in the interests of the two men. Bradford puts his first interest in the community, the covenant of men working together in common bond for a common purpose. But his Puritan community in America was soon broken apart, as he lived to see, by the pressures of the single individual striking out for himself. And it is in this single, isolated individual that Thomas Wolfe puts his first interest. In fact, *Look Homeward, Angel,* in company with Wolfe's later novels, is one long shout of exaltation of the individual standing lost but glorious against the community that would deny his isolated grandeur. Society, fellows, family serve only as the opponent, the common enemy of the embattled individual who refuses to surrender to conformity and loss of individualism. Like Eugene Gant himself, the single individual looms larger than life, striding through the wash of smaller men who have sold out to the crowd.

If the description sounds like a twentieth century commencement address exhorting the young to resist the conformity of their times, the impression may explain part of the failure of the novel. But it also explains part of the attraction of the novel for the American who from the beginning has been forced to meet the problem of the conflicting claims of his individualism and his community of fellows. And always the strong individual, standing alone and glorious, has been a favorite subject for the novelist. But the subject is capable of subtle as well as powerful handling, as a look at almost any of the great American novels will show. *Look Homeward, Angel* is a strident introduction to the theme, but only an introduction. Other and greater novelists have seen that Bradford's ideas are, after all, not so contemptible in a land that Bradford's ideas helped to found, and that Wolfe's gigantic individual must somehow live in this land amid these ideas and find his answer there.

The theme of isolation illustrated and dramatized in the one mighty individual is common to almost all of the great novels discussed here. Certainly *Huckleberry Finn* and *My Antonia* belong as clearly to the category as *Look Homeward, Angel* or any other novel that might be chosen. In a sense it is not a category at all, for with the exception of a few novels—particularly in the twentieth century—that concern themselves primarily with man in the group, the novel has always tended to concentrate on the individual. Such concentration is inevitable; a limited number of characters offers greater intensity and greater opportunity for detailed analysis.

More important, the individual reader is likely to be much more interested in other individuals than in men in a group or in society in general, and the whole intellectual atmosphere before 1900 was one that placed the highest importance on the individual. And since isolation and loneliness are by their very nature individual problems, although also by their nature they must concern man in relationship to his fellows, the novels that pursue the theme must concentrate upon the individual in relationship to those around him. If the American reader is to identify the problems of his own life with those of a fictional character, and so recognize immediately the relevance of the novel to his own existence, he needs individual characters that he may come to know and to understand. The great American novel, identified as it is with American life, has always wanted to give him the opportunity.

The novel of the frontier in particular must be a novel about the individual, simply because the frontier put its greatest stress on the individual. But the theme of isolation on the frontier is no different in nature from the theme when concerned with other conditions. Wolfe's lonely youth faces the same questions that Huck Finn faces, and must solve the same problems that Ántonia Shimerda or even the Deerslayer solve, however different the setting or the thematic conclusion may be. The novel of the frontier, like the frontier itself in American history, posed the problem of isolation for the American with imaginative as well as with historical immediacy. The frontier was there, a dramatic setting or situation available ready-made to the novelist, almost without his seeking, that could catch up and summarize the American experience, whether that experience was in fact concerned with the literal frontier or not. And over the years the novel of the frontier gradually reached a conclusion to the theme of isolation, an answer, a way of thought, an attitude, that was valid for the isolation of the frontier. It also proved valid for the theme when not directly concerned with the frontier, just as the novels were themselves relevant to the American experience behind the frontier as well as on it. Many of the greatest and most admired novels continued and deepened the theme and its conclusion, but they concentrated on the all-important individual in any situation rather than on the particular and defining situation of the frontier. As Bradford's history itself shows, it is man meeting his representative experience that is of thematic importance, not the setting for that meeting.

Nathaniel Hawthorne's *The Scarlet Letter* is not only one of the unquestionably great American novels; it is an equally great illustration of the mighty individual meeting his representative experience, fittingly in the same early days of Massachusetts that Bradford describes. It even catches something of the air of the frontier novel and so provides a convenient transition within the theme: the threatening presence of the forest all about the tiny town continually reminds the reader that this is a new settlement on a new frontier. Yet it is not a new life in the sense of the "beginning again" of the frontier; the temptations and challenges of Hester Prynne and Arthur Dimmesdale and Roger Chillingworth are the old temptations simply placed in a new setting. The forest is there, but not as a means of escape or a threat of isolation. It gives the impression more accurately of a wall or a barrier closing off the little settlement, making it a highly restricted scene in which the drama must be played out. The drama itself is representative, almost symbolic, of human nature anywhere and at any time; Hester Prynne is the powerful human being rather than simply a woman on the frontier. The theme of isolation in the novel is as relevant to the twentieth century as to the seventeenth where it finds its setting and to the nineteenth when it was written, for the isolated individual, whatever the immediate situation, belongs to one century as much as to another.

In particular, *The Scarlet Letter* has long held the American imagination as a study in the universal effects of sin on the individual human consciousness. In consequence, and perhaps more broadly, the novel is a study of human isolation, of the lonely individual and his relationship with his fellow beings, with his God, and, in a sense, with himself. For the element of isolation with which Hawthorne is most concerned here is the consciousness of sin, particularly of pride and its relationship to the general problem of human isolation, all illustrated in the one powerful individual. By thus broadening its base of human interest, although concentrating on the single scene and character, the novel is even more unlimited in its applicability. Even the symbolic and historical nature of Hawthorne's imagination cannot dim the immediacy of the character or the theme conveyed through the character. Bradford wrote of the same restricted Puritan world of *The Scarlet Letter*—although a real one rather than a symbolic one—but his history, like the novel, is as relevant now as then. Since in America the challenge of isolation has always been an especially pressing one, it is no wonder that *The Scarlet Letter* immediately caught the American imagination and has firmly held it ever since.

To show how clearly and how successfully *The Scarlet Letter* presents the theme of human isolation and in turn depends upon it for emotional and intellectual impact, the novel may be interpreted almost entirely in terms of human isolation and thus be placed clearly in the American tradition of the theme. It would not be misleading. Hester Prynne, Dimmesdale, and Chillingworth are defined by means of their relationship to society and to each other, and then eventually by their own view of themselves in this multiple relationship. The result is that, physically and emotionally isolated though they are, no one of them is ever allowed to live a completely self-contained existence, not even in his most private relationship with God or in his personal self-evaluation. For this is a world of ethical and religious consciousness in which they live, a world in which charity and love of fellow man is a necessary element of being, even at the moment when it may most completely be forgotten or ignored. And historically, too, this is the world of early colonial America, when a small group of people are huddled together in a community isolation, banded together necessarily in defense against the threat of the wilderness and the devil. Isolation, then, for these central characters is a matter, not simply of separateness itself, but of separateness from something, from their fellows, from each other, from a wholeness and harmony of self in the universe.

In an allegorical novel of the sure skill of *The Scarlet Letter* it is fitting that the central theme of isolation should find embodiment in a series of almost symbolic objects and situations. In a sense, of course, the characters themselves are such "objects," although the immediate effect they convey of living beings makes them much more. But in less important examples the novel presents a number of allegorical statements of theme. From the solitary wild rose bush growing in the weeds before the prison door to Hester Prynne's cottage on the remote edge of town away from other houses, the novel offers a number of "types" (as the Puritans called such symbols or allegorical emblems) of the isolation of the characters.

Rising above lesser objects, two large symbols seem to tower above the novel. The scaffold on which Hester first appears for public punishment, on which Dimmesdale makes his futile private confession, and on which he finally blurts out his public confession and dies, is a central image of the story. Here wrongdoers are separated from their fellows, literally and figuratively, and made to face their punishment alone. But behind even the scaffold is the colony itself, a tiny isolated strip hacked out of the wilderness, holding its inhabitants separate from the world. Only an occasional ship provides a hazardous communication with the outside, and Hester and Dimmesdale are denied even this ship. On one side is the sea, forbidding return to the past, and on all other sides is the wilderness forest: "This hemmed it in so narrowly, and stood so black and dense on either side, . . . that, to Hester's mind, it imaged not amiss the moral wilderness in which she had so long been wandering." [222] [2] Governor Bradford's powerful description of the first landing at Plymouth, the wilderness before and the sea behind, seems almost a source for the novel. Hawthorne's imagination, akin to the symbolic imagination of Bradford's Puritans themselves, sees the world of his story as a series of types or images, and presents his theme of isolation by indirection as well as by the direction of character and action.

Hester, Dimmesdale, and Chillingworth, however, are the center of the novel, and it is their characters and fortunes that make the allegorical background of interest. Each is introduced immediately as a figure in isolation from society. The first impression of Roger Chillingworth, standing in the crowd watching Hester on the scaffold, is of "a man chiefly accustomed to look inward, and to whom external matters are of little value and import." [72] Soon afterward, in the first interview with Hester, he reveals that he, "a wanderer, and isolated from human interests," [90] had married Hester to try to find some warmth of heart, some intimate companionship, in a chill and lonely world. The marriage had simply made his isolation greater. As his character degenerates in hatred and self-centered desire for revenge, even the im-

[2] Page references are to Nathaniel Hawthorne, *The Scarlet Letter, a Romance* (Boston: Ticknor, Reed, and Fields, 1850).

personal society around him begins instinctively to draw
back from the horror of his face. He is the greatest physician
in the tiny colony and was immediately accepted for his
learning and his ability, but as his character becomes in-
tuitively evident the acceptance becomes more and more
external, more a matter of necessity and physical advantage
than of personal warmth. Just as he rejects any love of
fellow man, even while ironically offering physical comfort and healing, he is rejected by his fellow man and left the
isolated wanderer he was in the beginning.

The Reverend Arthur Dimmesdale, too, is first seen, even
from outside, as "a being who felt himself quite astray and
at a loss in the pathway of human existence, and could only
be at ease in some seclusion of his own." [79] Yet his sense
of estrangement comes only from within, for he is one of
the most beloved of the ministers and is surrounded by
faithful parishioners. For many, particularly the younger
maidens of his congregation, he is a figure of human love as
well as of Godly love. Yet Dimmesdale is caught in a racking
quandary: he feels strongly the need for Christian charity,
and works toward love for his flock as well as love for its
spiritual well-being, even though suspicious of all mankind
and "trusting no man as his friend." [156] Much of this
loneliness comes, of course, from the sensitive consciousness
of his own sinful state that he feels alienating him from
those around him. His burden, paradoxically, gives him an
intimate sympathy with the equally burdened men about
him, yet forces him to keep a distance from them. One of the
horrors of evil here is that it prevents any real communication
of man with man. But Dimmesdale is by nature, too, a recluse,
unable and unwilling to open himself to others. In his union
with Hester, this quality creates much of the tragedy of the
novel; in his relationship with the world, it creates pathos
mingled with contempt. For Dimmesdale is a lonely man,

even when surrounded by love, and cannot force himself to
return the love to others. Just as it is ironic that Chillingworth is a physician, so it is ironic that Dimmesdale is a
Christian pastor. For he can take love and trust from his
flock but cannot give love or trust in return.

From her first appearance Hester Prynne, the towering
central figure, is a woman set apart. As she stands on the scaffold she is above the crowd, the center of all eyes, in the
midst of the people but not of them. To the end of the novel
she lives this life of conscious isolation, unpitied and un-
accepted. Even in the midst of the community she is banished
from it. Neither Chillingworth nor Dimmesdale ever knows
this sort of hopeless isolation, cut off from sympathy as well
as from affection, an outcast in the community. Yet Hester
is unlike either of them, for her isolation is imposed from
outside. She is neither incapable of love nor unwilling to
give it; she is simply unable to find a recipient. Unlike her
former husband Chillingworth, she does not ignore the need
for love toward others, and unlike her former lover Dimmesdale—lover only in the most restricted of meanings—she does
not find it impossible to give love to others. Indeed, once the
first shock of banishment and public shame is over, Hester de-
votes herself to service to others, to charity in act and deed.
Over the years she becomes known to the village for her
generosity of hand and heart, her willingness to give of
herself when needed. Still living in her circle of isolation, she
reaches out of it when it is for the good of others. And since
she is living in the midst of human beings, though Puritans
with a strict sense of their own justice, the circle becomes
less and less restricting as normal human affection comes into
play. To the very end, when she voluntarily returns to her
solitary life in the colony, there is still nothing that makes her
feel that she again belongs completely to human society in
this little outpost, but at least her exercise of charity, in

its fullest sense, has brought her back from the despair of the scaffold to the hopeful company of men.

Although Hester's external isolation from society, her rejection from the everyday life and thoughtless affection of the community, is lessened through the action of time and her own unassuming and generous deeds, this outward isolation is unimportant to her in comparison with the inner isolation which it has caused. The scarlet letter itself has forced her into a far deeper isolation: "It had the effect of a spell, taking her out of the ordinary relations with humanity, and enclosing her in a sphere by herself." [64] It is this deeper loneliness, where her shame and her baby and her scarlet letter are her only realities, that sets her off in real isolation from society. Here is the inner loneliness that is more difficult to fight, the separation from mankind that is potentially withering. Her first response, on the scaffold as afterwards, is to create "a stony crust of insensibility" [82], a refusal to let the outer world reach the center of her being. To break through this self-created defense and reach out into the world again then becomes a matter not simply of her relationship to others but to herself and to God. Like Chillingworth and Dimmesdale, Hester, too, lives in a self-created isolation, but one whose creation was forced on her from without. And her response to this loneliness is one entirely different from theirs.

The relationship of the central characters to the people about them is a part of the total dramatic structure of the novel, but the greater interest and most of the dramatic conflict lie in the relationship between the characters themselves. Of course the two sets of relationships are eventually one: Chillingworth's response to Hester or to Dimmesdale, for instance, is a part of his response to the world itself. He had originally married Hester to escape his isolation in the world, and so their union becomes a reflection or a product of his view of mankind. And just as Chillingworth is unable to defeat his egotism and reach out to the world, he is unable to defeat his pride and extend love and forgiveness to Hester. From his first view of her on the scaffold he instinctively rejects any thought of charity or of love, simply retiring into his shell of hatred. By the time of their final meeting in the forest Chillingworth has so degenerated that the two can hardly communicate. Hester, in contrast, is increasingly able to extend pity:

"What see you in my face," asked the physician, "that you look at it so earnestly?"
"Something that would make me weep, if there were any tears bitter enough for it," answered she. [205]

But Chillingworth has none to offer beyond a momentary thrill of admiration that is reminiscent of Milton's Satan standing "stupidly good" at the sight of Eve. Now at last he can even admit that he has been enjoying revenge on Hester too:

"Why hast thou not avenged thyself on me?"
"I have left thee to the scarlet letter," replied Roger Chillingworth. "If that have not avenged me, I can do no more!"
He laid his finger on it, with a smile. [209]

Apparently never a man of warmth or affection, he has been brought by his self-pity and his egotistical pride to the isolation of hell itself. And, what is worse, he tries to pull Dimmesdale and Hester in with him.

Hester can resist him, for she possesses the charity and the humility of acceptance of self to defend her. Arthur Dimmesdale has neither in any real sense, and he falls a victim all too easily. Mistrusting both mankind and himself, he is an easy target; and Chillingworth's revenge is one of the most dramatic—almost melodramatic—elements of the novel. As Chillingworth devilishly worms his way into Dimmes-

dale's heart, only to eat it out in vengeance, the reader squirms
with the tortured minister. The irony is too painful; the man
who will trust no one else trusts the one man who is his
enemy: "All that guilty sorrow, hidden from the world,
whose great heart would have pitied and forgiven, to be revealed to him, the Pitiless, to him, the Unforgiving!" [167]
Dimmesdale's tortured isolation, the one defense that he can
stupidly offer against the pangs of conscience, is itself the
cause of his final destruction. Chillingworth, even in the evil
of his burning hatred, is always coldly rational enough to see
the cringing weakness of Dimmesdale and to take advantage
of it. There is much to dislike in the minister, but he does
engender the pathos of passive suffering. Chillingworth in
the relationship, whatever his original provocation, is actively
evil: " 'That old man's revenge has been blacker than my
sin. He has violated, in cold blood, the sanctity of a human
heart. Thou and I, Hester, never did so!' " [237]

Dimmesdale and Hester Prynne have never committed an
active evil—beyond perhaps the single adulterous act that
precedes the novel, and it was relatively venial—for their
relationship is an entirely different one. Again two isolated
humans are brought together, again one passive and the other
active. But the active nature of Hester is one of love and
charity rather than pride and hatred. Dimmesdale, however,
is still crippled by his inability to give anything of the small
self hidden in the circle of his loneliness. It is a wonder that
he ever brought himself to love Hester even momentarily, and
one understands even more clearly why with instinctive art
Hawthorne makes no attempt to picture their earlier relationship. Through the story given, Dimmesdale holds himself
aloof from Hester, helpless and hopeless in his own loneliness
and consciousness of sin, but unwilling to endanger his position by helping her, and unable even to attempt to reach out
to her in secret. Even during the few moments on the scaffold

with her, hidden from the eyes of man, and the few moments in the forest, equally secret and hidden, when he feels some easing of his loneliness and suffering, some understanding and communication, he is careful to keep it so private that he simply draws Hester into his own isolation, taking from her but giving nothing in return. And then the moment of real tragedy in the novel, the complete finality of end, comes on the morning of his Election Day sermon when in his selfish and isolated preoccupation with his sermon—again the bitter irony—he can forget their moment of communication, forget their plans for escape together, ignore Hester herself, to take his hour of egocentric triumph. Hester, looking on, at last understands the true nature of their relationship:

Her spirit sank with the idea that all must have been a delusion, and that, vividly as she had dreamed it, there could be no real bond betwixt the clergyman and herself. And thus much of woman was there in Hester, that she could scarcely forgive him . . . for being able so completely to withdraw himself from their mutual world; while she groped darkly, and stretched forth her cold hands, and found him not. [292–93]

Dimmesdale at last is isolated even from the one capable of loving him—and doesn't care. His long delayed public confession is, then, only an anticlimactic gesture, without value and without meaning. He has so cut himself off from humanity that his public confession is as empty a gesture as his private one.

The moment on the scaffold, after Dimmesdale had tried to quiet his conscience by the confession in words but not in spirit or in honesty, when the minister takes the hand of Hester and little Pearl and feels a tumultuous rush of life other than his own pouring into his heart, is the moment that defines part of the relationship between the two. For Hester, even in her isolation, is, like Willa Cather's Ántonia, a source of

life and compassion and love, vital enough to transmit something of herself to him. And Dimmesdale, lonely, suffering,
cowardly, is willing to take from her so long as it does not
endanger him. This pattern is repeated at greater length in the
forest. Here Hester approaches him, offers again the mutual
understanding and love, and nerves him momentarily to a
plan to escape from the colony. Dimmesdale expands in her
warmth and with the loss of isolation begins to regain something of his old spirit and self-respect. Even her knowledge of
his sinful state, the secret that he wants to make public but
does not dare, is a partial escape from his brooding isolation:
" 'Thou little knowest what a relief it is, after the torment of
a seven years' cheat, to look into an eye that recognizes me for
what I am!' " [233] He thinks of himself with exhilaration as
"a prisoner just escaped from the dungeon of his own heart."
[246] But the reader as well as Hester soon discovers that he
has not escaped from his own heart, for this is the source of
corruption that he cannot escape. It comes as no surprise
that throughout the forest meeting Dimmesdale, so conscious
of the effect of corruption of heart on himself, never once
thinks of its effect on Hester. He has found momentary release from the isolation of his conscience but never from the
corruption of his heart. He remains as self-centered, as selfish
as ever, and in keeping with his character has been taking con-
solation from Hester, leaving her to find her own as best she
can. That she does find it, and can for a moment throw away
the scarlet letter and resume her role in the symbolic sunlight
as a full, vital woman, is more nearly a mark of her own
strength than of any change in the relationship between
them.

Hester's release and restoration, short-lived though it is—
in the forest little Pearl even brings back the scarlet letter that
Hester had thrown away, and immediately brings back with
it the gloom of the forest—is a mark, too, of the difference

between her strong character and that of the two men. For Hester does find escape from the circle of her isolation, or at least makes the circle so large that it allows a meaningful freedom within it, whereas the others never do. Certainly Chillingworth never does, but rather increasingly tightens his circle until there is nothing left inside but hatred. As the center of his existence becomes smaller and uglier, so in this allegorical novel he finally shrivels up and passes from human sight.

The Reverend Mr. Dimmesdale offers a more interesting case. "Case" is the right word, for Hawthorne makes him almost a case study—even though an allegorical one—of moral and psychological weakness in isolation. Yet it is a part of the praise of Hawthorne that we suffer with Dimmesdale as a man even while we watch him as an allegorical embodiment of ourselves as men. As a minister he knows the only valid answer to the problem of his conscience: confession and repentance and faith. But his moral weakness forbids him the answer. He makes the gestures, of course, but the gestures are meaningless. He confesses on the public scaffold, but at night when no one can hear; he insists in the pulpit on his sinfulness, but in such a manner that no one believes him. He repents bitterly and alone, but not enough to accept the results of his act. He has no faith in man, and as far as can be seen, little faith in God. The only answer that he can fully accept is to creep into his prison of isolation, further into his own self and further away from the liberating God whom he professes. *The Scarlet Letter* is inevitably a novel firmly grounded in the Christian belief; and it is this belief that Dimmesdale rejects even while longing for it. For the Christian, isolation from man may be painful enough, but voluntary isolation from God is unendurable. Dimmesdale, after painfully preserving it as long as possible, finally abandons his isolation through sheer weakness. But by then the element of free choice is gone, and he stands in public as isolated and as damned as he had stood in private, unable even at the end to escape completely from his petty self.

The real victory of Hester Prynne is that she does escape from self, so that even though still partially isolated from the community and still unable to find any meaningful communication or understanding with her husband or her lover, she does escape that blighting inner isolation from man and from God. She never denies her greater potentialities, spiritual or physical, to imprison herself in an isolation of mere hopelessness and bitter introspection. In a sense Hester is fortunate, of course, for she has no public confession to make; it is made for her, and in the most painful manner. Yet by her refusal to hide from the community, her refusal to excuse her actions or to minimize them, she continues to make her confession from her own heart and mind. It is true that for a while she is driven from the life of the community and into a defensive inner shell of isolation, but she never withdraws from man or from life itself. Her very confession forbids such a withdrawal, and her recognition and acceptance of her state of sinful knowledge even give her a greater understanding of those about her. Her scarlet letter is a bridge as well as a barrier: "She shuddered to believe, yet could not help believing, that it gave her a sympathetic knowledge of the hidden sin in other hearts." [102] In public, her confession and her acceptance of the error of the past take the form of service to humanity. Before too long the townspeople begin to think of her scarlet letter as standing for "Able." In private, she continues to feel a sympathetic bond with Dimmesdale and even to feel a responsibility for him. She never abandons him, as he does her, but offers her strength and her warmth where possible. And most important, at heart she keeps her vital flame alive and burning for others to see. There is no escapism here, no hiding of the soul, no withdrawal into the silent, secret life, but an openness and an honesty that parallel the confession itself. Hester does not withdraw from life, for that is not her nature. She is a full-blooded woman, placed almost incongruously in a group of scholars and ascetics. She is a reminder that the early Puritans were, after all, Elizabethan Englishmen and did not automatically lose their zest for life. She is penitent but not regretful, and when she sees the chance to escape with Dimmesdale to a better life she tries to grasp it. It is fitting that with the emotional release of throwing away the scarlet letter (itself so vividly embroidered) she regains much of her physical beauty. She is no angel on earth, no pious recluse lost in religious introspection, but a vigorous figure living this life in an honest role. And this turning outward to the full life makes her no less a Christian. When Dimmesdale in the forest feels a strange glow at the thought of escape from the colony and from himself, his response is hardly a religious one: "It was the exhilarating effect . . . of breathing the wild, free atmosphere of an unredeemed, unchristianized, lawless region." [246] But this is his, not Hester's, feeling. She has escaped from the "dungeon of her heart," but to a world of greater law, a world in which she can be redeemed in the midst of a full life. Her escape from inner isolation is not an escape *from* the Christian life but an escape *to* it, not a withdrawal *from* love and commitment but a move *toward* them.

It is just this difference in response to life and to self that makes the difference in the major characters. In a more worldly sense it is a difference in the human heart. In the allegorical manner in which the word is generally used, Chillingworth has no heart, and Dimmesdale suppresses his. But Hester is all heart, for she has purged hers of the evil that hardens and destroys. She is not at war with the world or with herself; the novel in fact makes it clear that eventually such a war is the greatest evil into which man can let himself fall.

Hawthorne clarifies the state of her heart by contrasting it with that of little Pearl, the strange allegorical child who seems to stand for the offspring of evil and is a living symbol of the scarlet letter. In her lonely amusements—and Pearl in her childish way is as isolated as anyone in the novel—she likes to create imaginary playmates:

The singularity lay in the hostile feelings with which the child regarded all these offspring of her own heart and mind. She never created a friend, but seemed always to be sowing broadcast the dragon's teeth, whence sprung a harvest of armed enemies, against whom she rushed to battle. It was inexpressibly sad—then what depth of sorrow to a mother, who felt in her own heart the cause!—to observe, in one so young, this constant recognition of an adverse world. [113]

It is particularly sorrowful to Hester, for she has been, in some respects like Eve, a carrier of evil, one capable of passing evil on, even though she has succeeded in defeating in her own heart the hatred and resentment of life and the world that are the mark of evil and isolation.

The modern psychological jargon would say that Hester is, or at least becomes, well adjusted in her world, even in her enforced isolation. But the older terms are more fitting to this novel and more accurate: Hester finally achieves the one great quality that is her salvation both now and after, humility. For Hester slowly reaches, through effort and through grace, the freedom from unwarranted pride of self, the ability to see her state in proper relation to man and to God, that is the only possible answer to the problem of sin and isolation set by the novel. This is the answer that Chillingworth and Dimmesdale cannot find or will not accept. Chillingworth, that almost allegorical Vice figure, tries to make himself superior to others, even to feed on the heart of another, to reach the revenge that his hatred demands. Dimmesdale will not accept himself for what he is, and alternately debases himself in an abject spiritual despondency that is almost a bitter parody of religious purgation or prides himself paradoxically on his worldly state. Only Hester can accept herself, what she has done and what she is, and then set about making the best of that self. Humility does not mean timid submissiveness or loss of self-respect; she endures, in the worldly sense, as a proud woman without regret and without shame. She does find that positive quality that can lift her out of despondency and self-deprecation as well as out of a proud conviction of superiority. This kind of genuine humility—even humanity—saves Hester from the sense of spiritual isolation, the feeling that she is cut off from mankind by anything more than a superficial view, for it restores her spiritually to humanity and her proper place in it. One result is the love that she is able to offer others, the affection and the service she gives to her fellow man. The important result is that she, alone among the major characters of the novel, is the only one not truly isolated from the world, from her fellow beings, or from herself, even though she is the one who would seem to have the greatest cause to be. In her humility she is the answer, Hawthorne would seem to say, to the torture of human isolation. The solution is neither an easy one nor always a pleasant one, but it is a valid one. Hester Prynne stands in proof.

Hester's answer is phrased in almost theological terms, a terminology that is rejected by most other American novelists not brought up in the early New England air. Hawthorne and Governor Bradford speak much the same language—particularly fitting here, of course, where the novel is set in Bradford's times—but, more important, they agree on the principles at work in the question of human isolation. Hawthorne's solution is Bradford's too, illustrated in the imagination rather than the historical vision, although Hawthorne's imagination incorporates an awareness of historical tradition that is kin to Bradford's. The solution is a long way from

the agonized self-pity of a Eugene Gant in content or in expression. But Hawthorne stands with the majority of fellow
novelists in content. Twain or Willa Cather or Salinger might
never use his terms—might even be repelled by them—but
they agree with his idea. Henry James, who at first glance
seems so different from these others, belongs to the same company, although he also would have been embarrassed to use
the religious terms of a Hawthorne or a Bradford. Then, too,
if *The Scarlet Letter* still has the setting and something of the
air of the frontier novel, James's *The Portrait of a Lady* has
the setting and the air of high civilization and sophistication.
England and Italy, the social graces and a wealthy civilization, seem a long way from the pioneer settlement of the
Massachusetts Bay Colony, and yet in James's novel human
life and isolation still lead to the same conclusion. Henry
James owed many critical debts to Hawthorne and the whole
tradition of the American novel; in his consideration of the
theme of human isolation he remains, if not in debt, at least
in agreement, despite any difference in the terms he uses to
express that agreement.

When Isabel Archer of *The Portrait of a Lady* is first discovered in her deserted house alone with a book she is about
to begin a career of isolation that, like Hester Prynne's, will
illustrate the full moral potentialities of the lonely mind. She
begins as a girl alone in the world and ends as a woman alone,
and her inner life of thought, feeling, instinctive responses,
and moral speculations is the novel itself. Here, again, is the
powerful individual who must face her problems alone. The
story is set in Europe, but it is an American story nevertheless,
and the European background makes Isabel's character, so
meaningful for the American experience and growing directly from the American mind, stand out all the more.
Throughout the novel she is surrounded by Americans, on the
one extreme side those who have become thoroughly Euro-

peanized, and on the other those who resist Europe with all their might, trying to retain a one hundred per cent Americanism that is as artificial as the life of the expatriates. The result is eventually an emotional isolation for Isabel, who refuses to go to one extreme or the other but would keep her American quality without self-consciousness and without shame. The result, too, for the reader is a story that he recognizes as an American one; that is, one that speaks to the American mind and experience, and is particularly meaningful to the American reader. Concerned as the novel is with the problem of human isolation, and especially the concomitant moral problem, *The Portrait of a Lady* is firmly set in the American experience.

Isabel arrives in Europe as a penniless orphan "taken up" by her aunt, the Europeanized Mrs. Touchett, who neither fully understands nor fully approves of her. She is sparkling with life and desire for experience of the world. She is alone with the world before her, and she loves the position. A proposal of marriage from the attractive—and to the European most desirable—Lord Warburton does not even tempt her, for she values above all things her freedom from commitments: " 'If there is a thing in the world that I am fond of, . . . it is my personal independence.' " [139] [3] She is intelligent and she is sensitive, and life stretches before her as a joy to be pursued, an experience that is to fulfill all her hopes and her higher pleasures. And it would seem that she is right in her expectations. Only the lack of money prevents her from exercising her will on the future, and at the death of her uncle, following the generous pleas of her cousin Ralph, she has the money. To be rich, says Ralph, is to be able to fulfill one's imagination. He is fulfilling his own in making her rich, and she is about to begin fulfilling hers. Neither can yet know

[3] Page references are to Henry James, Jr., *The Portrait of a Lady* (Boston: Houghton Mifflin and Co., 1882).

that the quality of her imagination, the youth, the innocence, the high idealism, is to destroy itself and, if not to destroy her, at least to make her a woman quite different from what she had ever expected.

By refusing the hand of Lord Warburton, and later of Caspar Goodwood, Isabel had exercised for the first time her power of independence and found it pleasant. At the moment independence simply means being left to her own youthful imagination without check or hindrance either from without or from within:

"I love you, Isabel," said Miss Stackpole, with feeling.

"Well, if you love me, let me alone. I asked that of Mr. Goodwood, and I must also ask it of you."

"Take care you are not let alone too much."

"That is what Mr. Goodwood said to me. I told him I must take the risks." [144]

In a sense this desire for complete freedom is itself a form of isolation—reminiscent, not so oddly, of Huck Finn's—self-imposed and easily abandoned if the wish arises. As James points out too, it is a sort of pride, a self-sufficiency that denies the need for others: "It may be affirmed without delay that Isabel was probably very liable to the sin of self-esteem; she often surveyed with complacency the field of her own nature; . . . impulsively, she often admired herself." [41] But this sort of complacency is at best a venial pride, not the real evil of *The Scarlet Letter*, for it is simply the mark of her youth and her enthusiasm, and is a part of her charm. Certainly it is not a quality that she would consciously cultivate. "Poor Isabel found occasion to remind herself from time to time that she must not be too proud, and nothing could be more sincere than her prayer to be delivered from such a danger; for the isolation and loneliness of pride had for her mind the horror of a desert place." [95] Isabel's is simply a healthy American mind turned loose in the conventions and the social pressures of the European scene, and if it displays the American's self-complacency, it also displays the good will, the curiosity, the desire for self-improvement that can go with such a mild isolation.

Her pride even seems a kind of good when it is brought into contrast with the complete egocentricity of Gilbert Osmond, the coldly selfish dilettante that she finally marries, and the reader suddenly discovers that her youthful pride has been but an ironic preparation for the complete evil of his. Within the story the shock of contrast is an even greater one for Isabel, for she had assumed that she had found in him a voluntary isolation from the demands of the outer world that was like her own independence. She had thought that his withdrawal, his refusal of outer commitments, was also a sign of his search for the best in the future. But when it is too late, when she has married him and brought to him the aid of her love and her fortune, she finds that his isolation is simply a product of his complete selfishness, an utter disregard for anything that does not flatter and obey his self-centered will. In a sense perhaps this is like her own youthful pride, but her pride magnified a thousand times and shifted in object from hope of self-fulfillment in the future to contentment with self in the present.

Osmond's spiritual isolation is not a passing youthful phase but a settled, old conviction that removes him entirely from the company of moral decency. When he tells Isabel that being triumphant is "doing what you like" [270] we recognize the ironic echo of Isabel's youth, but it is an echo distorted almost beyond recognition. For Osmond quite literally does only what he likes, and what he likes is to impose his own selfish and corrupt personality on the world rather than to create a personality from the experiences of the world. It is no wonder that he is but a "sterile dilettante" [303], for he has withdrawn from the life of humanity to the life of the im-

personal esthetic. And Isabel finds too late that "to renounce
everything but Correggio" [232] is, for him at least, to renounce humanity itself. Osmond is completely isolated in his
own self-sufficiency, and for him the world exists, insofar as
it exists for him at all, only to recognize his own superiority.
When Isabel is drawn into this closed circle of isolation her
only function, as far as he is concerned, is to offer just this
recognition. When she refuses, the only response of which
he is capable is cold hatred not unlike the cold desire for revenge of a Roger Chillingworth. One is reminded again that
one evil leads to another, and that love of self, if allowed to
go unchecked, is a natural precursor of hatred of others.
James's likening of Osmond's egotism to "a serpent in a bank
of flowers" [376] seems particularly appropriate.

Osmond's spiritual isolation and Isabel's quite different sort
of isolation that is to follow her discovery of her husband's
character are set in contrast to a European background of
social relationships that would seem to deny any real isolation.
There man lives his own life, but lives it in continual close relationship with others. The whole social system is based upon
one's knowing his exact relationship to the others about him.
A few, like Lord Warburton, may make some gesture toward
social "liberalism," but at best it is only a gesture. A complete
self-sufficiency is possible only to the occasional eccentric—
and to the visiting American. Perhaps Madame Merle, the
American who has become even more European than the
Europeans themselves, best illustrates this social consciousness:

Her nature had been too much overlaid by custom and her angles
too much smoothed. She had become too flexible, too supple; she
was too finished, too civilised. She was, in a word, too perfectly
the social animal that man and woman are supposed to have been
intended to be. . . . Isabel found it difficult to think of Madame
Merle as an isolated figure; she existed only in her relations with
her fellow-mortals. [167]

But neither Isabel nor Osmond is a European, much as he
would like to be, and they must play out their tragic game
in a culture that isolates them even more.

The definition of Osmond's self-centered existence in contrast to its social setting is made specific in Ralph Touchett's
condemnation:

> "I think he's narrow, selfish. He takes himself so seriously!"
> "He has a great respect for himself; I don't blame him for that,"
> said Isabel. "It's the proper way to respect others."
> "Yes, but everything is relative; one ought to feel one's relations.
> I don't think Mr. Osmond does that." [302]

It is in her agreement with Ralph's position, although she does
not yet know it, that Isabel is to define the sort of life that she
finally accepts and to take her moral stand. But first she is
driven against her will into an isolation that cuts her off, however momentarily, from relations with others. It comes when
she finally realizes what she has done and what the consequences will be. At that moment the walls seem almost literally to close in upon her: she has followed Osmond into "the
mansion of his own habitation," and it is "the house of darkness, the house of dumbness, the house of suffocation." [375]
She is closed in by a rigid will, "shut up with an odour of
mould and decay." [377] Her problem now is, not to preserve a thoughtless independence, but to win independence
again on other grounds.

Her first response is to withdraw still further into her detachment, although not entirely for self-protection. Instinctively she thinks of others, and she cuts herself off from the
world as much to protect the feelings of others as to protect
her own. She, too, constructs a screen about herself, but a
screen only to keep her pain from hurting others who love
her. Ralph Touchett and Lord Warburton and Caspar Good-

wood and Henrietta Stackpole will never know, if she can help it, how much she has been suffering. Even her very detachment and withdrawal are a form of relationship with those she loves. But hiding from the world, however generous her motive, offers no permanent answer. At best it can be but a stopgap, a moment of transition between the isolation of her girlhood and the isolation of her maturity. It is this slow decision, this painful lonely moral choice, that constitutes the heart of the novel and makes *The Portrait of a Lady* one of the great novels about human isolation. For Isabel does face the problem squarely, however much she must grope for its solution, knowing that she must choose her own salvation within the limits of the isolation set by external circumstances and her own character.

One of the high points of the novel comes when Isabel, meditating alone before the fire one night, slowly comes to understand her situation: separated from the world and from her friends, married to a man who hates her and is trying to force her will to his, the hopes and easy ideals of youth gone. But with the greater understanding and the shocks it brings she also begins to find the character that is to be hers for the rest of her life, the character that is to defeat her spiritual isolation. It is suggested, this new character, even by the background of Rome, no longer a contrast but now a sympathetic setting:

She rested her weariness upon things that had crumbled for centuries and yet still were upright; she dropped her secret sadness into the silence of lonely places, where its very modern quality detached itself and grew objective, so that as she sat in a sun-warmed angle on a winter's day, or stood in a mouldy church to which no one came, she could almost smile at it and think of its smallness. Small it was, in the large Roman record, and her haunting sense of the continuity of the human lot easily carried her from the less to the greater. [454]

Her answer, then, is to be neither despair nor a surrender to her isolation, but, as slowly becomes apparent to her, a resolution to continue to live her life to its fullest, a deliberate choosing to join her lot to that of mankind. Osmond may cut her off from his fellows and from himself, but he can never isolate her from her sense of participation in life, from the sense of the continuity of the human lot.

The decision, even though Isabel might not recognize her attitude as a decision, has immediate corollaries. The first is a continued feeling for the human lot of others. As the reader looks back over the last half of the novel one of his strongest impressions is that of the love of Isabel for others, sometimes even approaching the heights of Christian charity, much as James might shy from the term. Her love for her friends continues, and the death of Ralph Touchett is a greater pain for her than for nearly anyone else in the novel. Perhaps her feeling for him is tempered by the love that she cannot give her husband—certainly Ralph was in love with her—but the fact remains that she is still capable of love and is not isolated from her human emotions.

Even Henrietta Stackpole, the lively and amusing American journalist loosed on Europe, can still find in Isabel all of the old friendship and affection, unsoured by Isabel's own bad fortune. Henrietta seems destined for a happy marriage with her tractable Englishman, and Isabel's feeling is one of joy and good will rather than envy. By the very end of the novel Isabel is even able to give the persistent Caspar Goodwood a sort of fascinated attention that might yet turn into something greater. If Henrietta's last words to Caspar, the last words of the novel, do not provide the conventional happy ending, at least they leave the hope of one for the future: " 'Look here, Mr. Goodwood,' she said; 'just you wait!' " [520]

These are all friendships that under normal circumstances at least would be easy to give. It would not be so easy to feel

charity toward Osmond's daughter Pansy, toward Madame
Merle, or, most of all, toward Osmond himself. Yet Isabel
does. As a girl, of course, Pansy is a pathetic little creature
calling silently for the love that her father will not give her.
Isabel immediately becomes more of a mother to her than
Pansy had ever known. When Isabel finally discovers the
truth, that Pansy is the child of Madame Merle and that
Madame Merle had tossed Isabel to Osmond partly for the
sake of the child, her feelings toward the girl do not change
in the least. She loves Pansy for herself, not for the use to
which she has been put. Pansy is a pathetic human being for
Isabel, not an object for selfish manipulation or for the "aes-
thetic relish" [309] that her father takes in her. Even more
admirable is the charity that Isabel extends to Madame Merle
after she discovers the duplicity of this pretended friend.
Isabel is hurt, of course, and even momentarily angry. Yet she
refuses to let anger or hatred seize her as it has Osmond;
revenge is not her business or her pleasure. It is even with a
certain sympathetic sadness that she tells Madame Merle in
the convent that she would like never to see her again. When
Mrs. Touchett asks Isabel at the end whether she still likes
Madame Merle, she can answer simply, " 'Not as I once did.
But it doesn't matter, for she is going to America,' " and then
add, even with a touch of humor, " 'She will make a con-
venience of America.' " [503] Her response is fully human
and one that recognizes the humanity in another.

Toward her husband Isabel's feelings are more complex,
but in essence they are not so very different. Once again her
final victory is one of charity over hatred. Osmond has hurt
her in the most cruel manner possible, not by any physical
act or by any open violence, but, like Chillingworth, by prey-
ing on her heart. He has literally used her for his own con-
venience, taking all and giving nothing, and finally he even
hates her for not being more useful for the cultivation of his

self-esteem. Isabel, however, does not, and even cannot, return hatred for hatred. She draws back from him as far as she can, of course, wrapping herself, like Hester Prynne, in a protective coat of isolation, and simply tries to live her own life as far as possible. She is no saint of heavenly love. Yet there is even in her detachment from him an element at least of forgiveness as she forces herself to believe that the situation is in part her own fault: "There were times when she almost pitied him; for if she had not deceived him in intention she understood how completely she must have done so in fact." [372] Here is an understanding, a sympathetic comprehension, that is far beyond anything he can offer or even imagine. Even in the relationship that is most hateful and most painful to her Isabel cannot escape her humanity.

The second corollary of Isabel's decision to devote herself to life rather than to the cultivation of a spiritual isolation is her increased sense of moral responsibility. In a way, of course, moral responsibility is simply another form of love of humanity, for it requires that others come before self. To do what one feels is right rather than to do only what one wants is the highest form of love for others. If the two coincide, the duty and the desire, one has reached the highest form of humanity. Isabel has reached no such exalted peak, but she does bring herself to the state of mind in which she unerringly chooses the right over the tempting desire. The result is a renewal of humanity, an increased feeling of her human relations, a form of the humility that Hawthorne had demanded, that constitutes a virtual denial of the isolation in which she is forced to live. By reaching out of her barrier of isolation, not to take, but to give, she destroys the barrier in all but a superficial sense. The comparison with Osmond, for whom "doing what you like" is the final triumph of man, is obvious. And it is fully within the bounds of psychological realism that at the end of the novel Osmond, like Chillingworth, is a lost man, trapped within his own self and damned in his spiritual isolation, while Isabel is saved for humanity, isolated only by external force, and leading a full human life that denies the isolation of self.

Isabel's most dramatic illustration of her inner conviction of moral responsibility is her decision to return to Osmond when she has physically at least escaped from him. There is every temptation to stay in England: her husband hates her, and she knows life with him will be one of silent suffering; he is far away and will not pursue her; she is surrounded now with affection and physical as well as mental comfort. Yet, like Hester Prynne, she does return, and the act makes her one of the great human beings, one of the mighty individuals, of fiction. In one sense, of course, it is an act of pride. Henrietta had earlier accused her of this:

> "You won't confess that you have made a mistake. You are too proud."
> "I don't know whether I am too proud. But I can't publish my mistake. I don't think that's decent. I would much rather die."
> [427]

If it is pride, it is an admirable one, for it is based not on self-love but on a very human sense of decency. And, more important, Isabel goes on to say to Henrietta: " 'One must accept one's deeds. I married him before all the world; I was perfectly free; it was impossible to do anything more deliberate.' " [428] Her pride is not in her self but in her responsibility to her obligations, to the consequences of her free choice of action. And such a responsibility is wholly praiseworthy. With the usual irony of the novel, Osmond a little later says almost the same thing: " 'I think we should accept the consequences of our actions, and what I value most in life is the honour of a thing!' " [471] But his sense of honor is the result not of a conviction of moral responsibility but

simply of what James calls "the observance of a magnificent
form." [472] The two states of mind, superficially alike, are
in reality far apart, for his is based on self-admiration and hers
on self-respect.

Isabel then returns to accept the consequences of the marriage to which she had freely committed herself. There is no
question in her mind: "Certain obligations were involved in
the very fact of marriage, and were quite independent of the
quantity of enjoyment extracted from it." [510] This is the
penalty of free will, but it is also the glory; the moral choice,
as James illustrates so dramatically, may also be the heroic
choice. In a way, too, her decision is again a result of her
sense of humanity. She owes a certain charity toward Osmond, little as she wants to give it. But, more important, she
has a debt of humanity to Pansy. Poor Pansy, caught between
the selfish ambitions of her father and the promptings of her
own heart, lost somewhere between the convent and two
parents who feel no love or responsibility for her, has only
Isabel to give her the love and the protection she needs. But
to help her Isabel must return to Osmond. On leaving Pansy
at the convent Isabel had promised never to desert her, and
she lives up to her promise. A love for Pansy, a responsibility
freely accepted, a moral obligation inherent in her humanity,
all draw Isabel back to the girl. She has no choice but to return to Italy, although the very lack of choice is itself a moral
choice of the highest order.

Her return is a matter of deliberate moral responsibility,
but it grows from her larger sense of participation in life,
her almost instinctive place in the continuity of the human
lot. Her feeling at the moment of decision is the true climax
of the novel:

It might be desirable to die; but this privilege was evidently to
be denied her. Deep in her soul—deeper than any appetite for
renunciation—was the sense that life would be her business for

a long time to come. And at moments there was something in-spiring, almost exhilarating, in the conviction. [492]

This is the choice of life over death, of participation over isolation, and mere suffering cannot touch it. With this exhil-aration she can return to Italy knowing that she has won the fight against spiritual isolation, against a lonely and lingering death in the self. "She should not escape; she should last." [492–93] There is something stubborn about life in her, more stubborn than her husband's selfishness or her own tempta-tions or the force of circumstances. Here is the genuine inde-pendence of mind that as a girl she had thought so easy to grasp. And it has turned out to be not a retreat from life but an approach, not a refusal of commitments but an acceptance of them. Committed so firmly and so stubbornly to life and the human lot, she can never be wholly isolated.

When Isabel first began to know Madame Merle—or at least to think that she did—she noticed that Madame Merle seemed to exist only within a social scene, and she soon began to wonder what she was like within herself: "Isabel often wondered what her relations might be with her own soul." [167] And behind the social scene, behind the relationship between the various characters, this is the central question of the novel itself. For it becomes increasingly clear as the novel progresses that the two relationships cannot be sep-arated. Like Hester Prynne, Isabel Archer discovers that the relationship with her own soul is the answer to the problem raised by her external isolation from others. By forgetting self in the dedication to a larger life the self is no longer iso-lated. In *The Scarlet Letter* the answer is made in religious terms: humility before God, the loss of selfish pride, is not to lose life but to find it. In *The Portrait of a Lady* the answer is made in moral terms: to forget one's self for the satisfaction of moral responsibility, to follow the difficult demands of human and humane morality rather than the easy temptations of human desires, is not to deny life but to affirm it. In the final analysis the two answers are the same. And the ending of the two novels is the same: both heroines—for they are heroic individuals—return by choice to a lonely and painful life. But in the very loneliness they have defeated the isolation of the spirit and have reached out from the dungeon of the heart to a larger life that will sustain them.

The novel of the frontier may have set out dramatically the problem of isolation in America and over the years may have offered the final conclusion within the theme. But the novel of the single powerful individual facing the problem and by sheer strength of character finding for himself the same conclusion brings the theme home to the American in a more personal and immediate form. Here is the one individual confronted by the American experience, and an experience not dramatically enforced by the physical isolation of the land itself, who arrives through his own efforts at the conclusion that seems eventually to satisfy and resolve the question of isolation for the American in any condition or situation. Thomas Wolfe may heighten and even exaggerate in his novel the plight of the lonely American, but Hawthorne and James in their quieter and more thoughtful way offer the resolution of that plight that seems to be the final resolution. Governor Bradford was one of the first to announce and defend it in America, and the majority of the great novelists who later took up the theme agreed with him in whatever terms or whatever dramatic situations caught their imagination and their understanding. Other novelists who followed Hawthorne and James were to develop the theme and its conclusion to suit the needs of the new American of the next century, but Hawthorne and James, with their portrayal of the single mighty individual, had already taken the theme out of the frontier and developed its question and its answer for the American anywhere and at any time.

IV

The Commonplace
and the Grotesque

One of the pleasures of William Dean Howells' *The Rise of Silas Lapham* is the recognition in it of the commonplace surface of American life, a pleasure that Howells helped to introduce to the American novel, defended in his criticism, and made—with others, of course—one of the characteristics of the novel to follow. The central character here, Silas Lapham, is by no means a common man, and the story of his life is not one that would be called common. Yet there is something recognizably commonplace in the character and the story, and much that the reader feels is familiar in the real world about him. There is nothing that could not conceivably happen, nothing to strain the imagination or to deny the familiar world. This impression of literalness and of the commonplace is presumably what Howells meant by the "realism" that he demanded in such critical works as *Criticism and Fiction* (1892). It does lead him to tell the story of a man whom we recognize as a believable American, and part of the believable American quality is the sense of isolation that the character must face. At the same time the commonplace quality forbids Howells to give Silas Lapham the heightened stature that would make him a great symbol of American isolation, as Hawthorne does, for instance, with Hester Prynne, or James with Isabel Archer. To deal with the commonplace does not mean, of course, to deal only with the surface. Silas Lapham exists as much in his inner life as he does in his outer. But it does mean that Howells had to limit himself to placing Lapham in a reasonably familiar predicament and then allowing him to extricate himself in a manner that is neither exaggerated nor unusually challenging. The result is a quiet story of a man dealing as best he can with familiar problems: there is no symbolic heightening of problem and solution, no universal answer to the American dilemma, but rather a narrative of a real man in a commonplace world. With *Silas Lapham* and the other "realistic" novels of its sort the continuing and steady theme of human isolation received another form and another expression in the American novel.

When the novel opens, Silas Lapham is a very successful business man, the owner of an expanding paint factory, and we recognize in him something of the familiar mild isolation into which enthusiasm for his business so often drives the American. At first, when Silas was just beginning the profitable exploitation of his original paint mine, he had gladly allowed his wife Persis to help him and to take a hand in affairs. But now that the business is thriving and he can afford to be without her in the office—or perhaps better, as he would put it, to relieve her of the burden—he is glad to run the business alone, even keeping her in ignorance of what he is doing. His ill-fated business partner Rogers, who is to contribute so much to his eventual ruin, he has long ago sloughed off. Now he can conduct his affairs with a lone hand, bothered by no one and responsible to no one. It is perhaps ironic that when he does finally go down to financial ruin it is partly because of the pressure that he cannot keep his wife from applying to his business conscience. But until that moment he presents a familiar picture to his family: " 'Oh, take a rest! The man slaves harder every year. It used to be so that he'd take a little time off now and then; but I declare, he hardly ever seems

to breathe now away from his office.' " [209] [1] As his affairs
grow steadily worse, so does his self-imposed isolation. He
brings home papers and works alone all night; he desperately
tries to recoup his fortunes without telling anyone of his
plight; he withdraws more and more into himself, partly to
save his family from worry, partly in pride and shame. It
is only complete failure that at last forces him out of his
business isloation and back into the arms of his family. And
then he is welcomed back as though from a long trip.

Although the story of Lapham's business affairs begins in
a tone of what might almost be called sympathetic derision,
it ends in a tone of serious concern as Howells begins to be
caught up himself in the problems of his character. The business world becomes eventually the world of moral concerns
in the novel, just as the social world is the moral world in
James's novels, and Howells begins to see in moral concerns
the traditional center of his novel, even though the decision
means dropping to some degree the tone of humane banter
with which he began.

But the story is also concerned with the socially naive business man and his family isolated in the midst of a sophisticated
Boston society—the American myth of Boston is fully ex-
ploited here—and the tone of this part of the story remains
lighter throughout the novel. Silas and Persis were born
country children in Vermont, and sudden wealth has changed
them very little. But with the wealth has come, almost against
their will, a vague social ambition: Silas has as much money as,
and more than, the socially accepted, so why shouldn't he
join their circle? And besides, there are always the children;
it would be only right to give them every opportunity. And
still further, since he is building a fine new house on the water
side of Beacon as a symbol of his success, why shouldn't they

[1] Page references are to William D. Howells, *The Rise of Silas Lapham*
(Boston: Ticknor and Co., 1885).

join the social life of their coming neighbors? Since Persis and the two girls, Irene and Pen, had some time before by a lucky accident made the acquaintance of the Coreys, who are completely acceptable in Boston, the way seems clear ahead. All of the family is in agreement, although no one wants to admit it at first, and they gradually begin to drift almost as if by accident toward the world of high society.

Unfortunately it is not a world eager to receive them. Howells derives a good deal of amusement from the accepted view of the proper Bostonian. When young Corey suggests that Lapham should be tested by other standards than Boston's, the elder Mr. Corey answers: " 'This comes of the error which I have often deprecated. . . . In fact I am always saying that the Bostonian ought never to leave Boston. Then he knows—and then only—that there can *be* no standard but ours.' " [89] Mr. Corey speaks with a chuckle, but the fact remains that Boston society does have its own code and its own values, and knows quite clearly what it expects from any new member:

"Society is a very different sort of thing from good sense and right ideas. It is based upon them, of course, but the airy, graceful, winning superstructure which we all know demands different qualities. Have your friends got these qualities,—which may be felt, but not defined?" [194]

The Laphams do not have the qualities, do not know what they are, and have no real desire to find them. And if young Corey and the Lapham girls were not coming so dangerously close to courtship, Boston could not care less.

Since Corey is courting one of the girls, however, and the Laphams are flirting at least with society, something has to be done. The Coreys give a formal dinner for the Laphams, and it is one of the high points of the novel. For days before the dinner the Laphams are at a painful loss to know how to dress and how to act, and when the fatal evening finally does arrive poor Silas knows that he is completely out of his element. The talk flows, as Corey would say, in an airy, graceful, winning style, and Silas understands none of it. The wine flows even more freely, and Silas, unused to wine with meals, gets drunker and drunker, talks louder and louder, and finally is all but carried home. It is an amusing episode, and a cruel one, and a pathetic one. And it is pathetic just because each side shows its best qualities but finds itself isolated from the other. When Lapham talks of his war experiences he brings into the dinner table conversation a strength and a depth at odds with the conversational froth that has gone before. The others know that they are dealing with a genuine man. On the other hand, the wit of the others and the concern with matters of intellect and taste show a culture and a grace that Lapham lacks. Then when Lapham grows too befuddled, the other men do show a forbearance and an understanding that is in keeping with their claims as "gentlemen." Neither really understands nor accepts the other, but Howells shows an admirable restraint in presenting both sides with sympathy and with fairness.

Even when Tom Corey finally marries Penelope Lapham, after a series of amusing misunderstandings about which of the two girls he loves, the circles of the Laphams and the Coreys hardly intersect. The two families belong to different worlds, and financial success or failure makes little difference; the Laphams remain as foreign to the world of the Coreys as ever. Young Tom's flash of instinctive contempt for Lapham after the dinner, and particularly after Lapham's apology, the result of a lifetime of social training for the boy, is an indication of the true width of the gulf between the two families. But again, the Coreys are not caricatures of the idle rich drawn from some melodrama of the time. Mr. Corey, in fact, is an amusing man whose taste and wit and good hu-

mor show some of the deficiencies of Lapham himself. It is
equally true, however, that with the reader's sympathies on
the side of the Laphams, the Coreys' almost unconscious
snobbery becomes more and more apparent—and more annoy-
ing. Mr. Corey's carefully treasured taste begins to look weak
and foolish before Lapham's strength of character, just as his
dilettantish idleness begins to cloy in the face of Lapham's
energetic struggle in the market place. Mrs. Corey is so completely the snob that in the long run she is more likable than
Mr. Corey, who at least is conscious, and at times even
ashamed, of his state of mind.

The important point, however, is not the quality of the
Coreys but the character of Silas Lapham's view of his relationship with them. And that relationship is summed up in his
face as he returns home after the visit of Mr. Corey to Lapham's office: "He was not letting his wife see in his averted
face the struggle that revealed itself there—the struggle of
stalwart achievement not to feel flattered at the notice of
sterile elegance, not to be sneakingly glad of its amiability, but
to stand up and look at it with eyes on the same level."
[203–4] But the battle for recognition is too great, taking
place, as it does, on the chosen field of the Coreys. Neither
man ever really understands the other, and Lapham cannot
bridge the gulf of training, custom, interests, personality, even
self-assessment, that enforces the isolation of social standing.
He has found something that he cannot buy, and if it is not
worth the buying—the source eventually of the humor—that
has nothing to do with the rejection that he meets.

When Silas comes home and tries to hide his feelings about
the Coreys from his wife, he is in one respect nearer the
center of interest of the novel than he is in his business struggle or in his social struggle as such. For *The Rise of Silas
Lapham* is essentially and centrally a story of family relationships. The novel is carefully plotted, almost too carefully, and

the various story lines are artfully interwoven: the story of Lapham's business fortunes and the story of Tom Corey's courtship of Penelope with all the misunderstandings and confusions that attend it. Each of the individual stories impinges on the others, modifying and influencing them. But, more important, each comes back directly to the Lapham family relationship, strengthening it, weakening it, testing it in one way or another. In one sense the novel is made up of a number of interrelated stories, but in another it is only one story, the story of the Lapham family and its response to a series of crises. Here in the family, too, is the center of the problem of isolation in the novel. For as long as the Lapham family is united in love and mutual dependence there can be no deep isolation for any member of it. The family as a whole may be isolated in the world, just as Ántonia's was to be in Willa Cather's novel, and in a certain sense is so by its own nature:

The very strength of their mutual affection was a barrier to worldly knowledge; they dressed for one another; they equipped their house for their own satisfaction; they lived richly to themselves, not because they were selfish, but because they did not know how to do otherwise. [35]

But such a tight circle of interdependence, as long as it is held intact, defeats the imposition of isolation from within or from without on any individual in the family. There can be no isolation from without, for the others are always there. There can be none from within, for each member of the family must be responsible to the others as well as to himself.

As long as it is united the Lapham family is one of the most charming and one of the most admirable in American literature. There is a positive pleasure in watching such a group of diverse individuals rub along together so well and in such good spirits. And the members are diverse: Silas is bluff and ambitious and hard working, while Persis provides the needed encouragement and at times the ethical conscience that Silas would like to ignore; Irene is quiet and dreamily romantic, while Pen is witty and detached. Together they complement each other, making up as a group for any quality they may lack as individuals. Their sense of humor, so often lacking in the dramatization of the theme of isolation, is perhaps their most notable common characteristic, and it keeps them in amity as much as any other quality. Pen teases Irene into good humor when needed, and Silas and Persis seldom consider any event without a certain dry Vermont joshing. It is high praise of Howells' ability that this good humor is neither forced nor artificial but seems to spring naturally from the common family love of the Laphams.

The picture of a happy family is particularly effective too in its contrast to the Coreys. There Mr. and Mrs. Corey seem as often separated as together, and young Tom is too often out of sympathy with them. There is humor in their family too, but Mrs. Corey does not share in it, and that makes all the difference. And, unlike the Laphams' easy and familiar joshing, the Corey humor is too often satiric and biting. The Coreys are by no means an unhappy family—Howells is too committed to the commonplace for such a violent contrast—but they do point up the particularly united and happy quality of the Laphams.

The failure of any real isolation of Silas Lapham in the social world, then, is that the family is united in the common experience. Conversely, his very real isolation in the business world is not simply that he tries to meet his problems alone but that he tries to meet them without the help or even the knowledge of the family. As he withdraws more and more into himself trying to recoup his lost fortunes he draws further and further away from his family. The strain tells on them all, as Silas grows moody and silent, and Persis hurt and suspicious. Then when the greatest test comes, the temptation to sell the mill that will save him but bilk the buyers—and the middlemen are perfectly willing and even anxious to be dishonest—he must meet the problem alone. This is his real moment of isolation. Further, the isolation is fortuitously deepened by other sources of discord in the family: Irene is off at the farm suffering from self-pity over the loss of Tom Corey to Pen, and Persis is so blind in her feeling of moral obligation to Rogers, now Silas' tempter and business enemy, that she cannot offer understanding or pity. But once Lapham has faced his moment and conquered it, preferring poverty to dishonesty, the family comes together again and Silas' isolation is a thing of the past. Now he can completely unburden himself to his wife; now she suddenly sees how her conscience has driven her on where her intelligence could not follow, and that her husband has been right all along; now Irene comes home again, ashamed of having abandoned the family when it needed her most. In one sense the family has been an index of Lapham's feeling of isolation, but in another and a more meaningful sense it has been the true origin of the feeling. When the family is together, emotionally and sympathetically, there can be no real isolation; when it is driven apart, only loneliness can follow.

The family is the primary factor in the novel, but an individual must still live with himself. In *The Rise of Silas Lapham* the relationship of the individual to his private conscience and the relationship to his family are so close and so interrelated that they cannot be completely separated; it is more than interesting that Silas sees the family reunited only after his conscience as well as Persis' is clear. It is fitting, for a man can surrender himself to others only when he has defeated the self-love that keeps him apart and that is the basis of the temptation to dishonesty. When Silas refuses

to sell the mill that he knows is worthless, he ensures his
financial ruin, but he also ensures the self-respect and the
respect of others that restore him to full participation in the
family.

In the shadow of his disaster they returned to something like
their old, united life; they were at least all together again; and it
will be intelligible to those whom life has blessed with vicissitude,
that Lapham should come home the evening after he had given
up everything to his creditors, and should sit down to his supper
so cheerful that Penelope could joke him in the old way.
[495–96]

And the family, united in love and respect, ready to face
the world again together, is the final triumph of Silas Lapham.
Back in Vermont, with even the fine new house on the
water side of Beacon burned to the ground, Silas has been
defeated by the business world and by the social world, but he
is neither lonely nor unhappy. Within the love of his family
he has defeated the true isolation that might have been
brought by loss of love and loss of self-respect.

It is the "rise" of Silas Lapham that he has come through
his ordeal "unscathed and unstained" [494], with his manhood restored. He is again complete, with his business life,
his social life, his family life all in union again, and all in
agreement with his moral instincts. In a way he has found
the same solution to the threat of isolation that Hester Prynne
and Isabel Archer found; he has suppressed the egocentric
desires of the self in favor of the demands of a greater
unselfish code. Yet Howells, firmly within the bounds of
the commonplace, cannot allow the solution to be so rigorous
or so heroic. Silas Lapham is an admirable man and a strong
man, but he is no hero, and if at the end he has done the right
thing and is restored to the completeness of manhood again,
he faces a future neither of great victory nor of great defeat.

There is even a puzzled disillusionment as Rogers accuses Silas of ruining him by his honesty: "This was his reward for standing firm for right and justice to his own destruction: to feel like a thief and a murderer." [468] And as Silas tries to begin his business enterprises again Persis notices in him "a daunted look that made her heart ache for him." [499] Lapham is a perfectly possible man, one who does not stretch the imagination of the reader unduly, and even his rise is one that might well occur in the real world of the American reader; one honest and moving but neither tragic nor heroic.

It is the very possibility of the story and the character, however, that gives both much of their strength. Silas Lapham meets the commonplace isolation that one might expect to meet, and finds the commonplace answer to it that one might conceivably have the strength of character to find. If neither the problem nor the answer is magnified and imaginatively heightened, they are nevertheless meaningful and firmly set in the American experience and the American tradition. For Howells is imaginatively concerned with the same sense of isolation that Hawthorne and James are concerned with. But in keeping with his literary theories (and, in a sense, his ethical too) he presents the same content in a different fictional manner, bringing the heightened and symbolic statement down, like Willa Cather or J. D. Salinger, to the commonplace life of a man and his family. In this sense historically he looks both backward and forward, in keeping with his accepted position as a transitional novelist. He concerns himself with the great common subject of human isolation, and he comes to the same conclusion—the need for an essentially moral answer—as many of those who wrote before him and after him. At the same time, like the novelists who followed him, he presents the concern and the answer in a picture of an ordinary family and of everyday life and everyday people as he deliberately writes in keeping with his comment in the story itself: " 'The novelist who could interpret the common feelings of commonplace people would have the answer to "the riddle of the painful earth" on his tongue.' " [285] The riddle and the solution that he presents are part of the great tradition of the American nineteenth century novel, but they look forward as well to the twentieth century yet to come.

The "common feelings of commonplace people" of the next century, however, were not quite those of a Howells, even though the theme of human isolation in American life and the American novel continued much the same. Certainly the intensity of interest in the theme was as great as, if not greater than, in the age of Howells. Sherwood Anderson's *Winesburg, Ohio*, as a representative example of the new novel, is a collection of interrelated sketches of isolated and lonely people in a small commonplace Ohio town, but people suffering a loneliness more intense than Howells would have allowed. A few have found contentment in their isolation. Joe Welling ("A Man of Ideas") is a happy man as he lives in his own world of ideas, and Tom Foster ("Drink") finds happiness by discovering the world in his own imagination. Most are unhappy in their isolation, and many have been warped and twisted by their experience. Seth Richmond ("The Thinker") is simply unhappy as he believes himself alone and unloved in the world, unable to recognize the love around him. Elmer Cowley ("Queer"), on the other hand, approaches madness in his conviction that the world finds him queer and that he must somehow "show them." Alice Hindman ("Adventure"), abandoned by her lover and refusing to give herself another, almost summarizes the plight of all: " 'What is the matter with me? I will do something dreadful if I am not careful,' she thought, and turning her face to the wall, began trying to force herself to face bravely the fact that many people must live and die alone, even in Winesburg." [134] [2]

Almost every one of the twenty-odd stories is concerned in one way or another with human isolation; one sketch is even called "Loneliness," and the word "lonely" occurs over and over again. Each character is somehow cut off from the world around him and is generally deeply troubled by the fact: "It seemed to her that between herself and all the other people in the world, a wall had been built up." [93]; Winesburg is a town of individuals who collide but never meet. Loneliness is the mark of mankind there, and each person must live his life alone within transparent walls that no one else can enter.

The walls seem transparent, however, only because Anderson is primarily concerned with the intense inner life of his characters, commonplace as they may appear on the surface, and uses every means to let this hidden life shine through. It is here that the novel begins to diverge from that of Howells. Wash Williams ("Respectability"), hurt by the world and consumed with hatred in his isolation, unburdens himself for the first time to George Willard, the young newspaper reporter who appears in all the sketches and whose story is the central one of the book. On the surface the method is reminiscent of the opening of *The Rise of Silas Lapham*, where Silas is interviewed by a reporter. But in Anderson's novel the reader is allowed to hear a story denied to the rest of the world, a story completely private and personal, and he knows the agonized thoughts of Wash Williams as no one else can know them. Howells would not be willing to be so frank, to go so deeply into the unconscious, or even to present such a disordered mind. Or, in another method of

[2] Page references are to Sherwood Anderson, *Winesburg, Ohio; a Group of Tales of Ohio Small Town Life* (New York: B. W. Huebsch, 1919). My thanks for copyright permission go to The Viking Press, Inc.

fictional presentation, the reader goes with the Reverend Curtis Hartman ("The Strength of God") as he sits in his lonely study in the bell tower of the church supposedly writing sermons but really staring with cupidity and guilty abandon at the bare shoulders and white throat of the woman behind the open window across the street. The reader hears his thoughts and knows his feelings as well as or better than the minister himself. Howells would not have allowed such feelings or presented them so frankly. It is this concern with the tortured inner life, with the secret thoughts and feelings, even the subconscious fears and desires of the many characters of the sketches, that places the stories so clearly in this century rather than in the age of Howells. The theme is the same, and the interest in the life of the commonplace person is the same, but the means of illustrating the theme and of presenting the character and his problem of isolation differ.

The novelists of the nineteenth century were, of course, equally concerned with the inner life of their characters, but they did not generally present it so directly and so openly. They tended at least to offer the character as he appeared to others, leaving to the reader's understanding and experience the comprehension of the hidden life that directed this outer appearance. As Henry James—one of the first novelists and one of the best to experiment with direct presentation of inner thoughts—kept insisting, the reader had to meet the author halfway, participating in the creative process himself. But Anderson, like so many of his fellow novelists more interested in the psychological state than in the physical, simply offers the psychological state directly and unmistakably.

Winesburg, Ohio is better characterized as a series of sketches than as a series of stories, for there is more interest in character than in plot, and the action is psychological action. Perhaps in the long run any such clear distinction is foolish; the lonely character in twentieth century fiction is no better known by the reader than the one in the nineteenth, and one sort of action is not in essentials so different from another. Character and plot, inner life and outer life can never be entirely distinguished from each other. But the new novelist could place his first emphasis on the inner rather than on the outer world and could introduce the reader there immediately. Sherwood Anderson did. The interest is an old and a constant one, but the fictional technique, so like the psychoanalytic technique just then becoming well known, was new in American fiction.

The growing popular interest in the new psychiatric knowledge was—and probably still is—predominantly in the study of the abnormal mind rather than the normal. And *Winesburg, Ohio* is full of sketches of abnormal minds, men and women driven into a warped and lonely isolation from the world and then made even more warped by the isolation itself. Even religion becomes fanaticism here, and Jesse Bentley ("Godliness," "Surrender," "Terror") thinks of himself as the Old Testament Jesse, a lonely founder of a new race, and sets himself apart from men. But the problem of isolation is itself not an abnormal one, and the total effect of the sketches is not one of abnormality for its own sake. Taken as a group, they simply present various aspects of the same problem, one in which the abnormal has its place. It is this common theme of human isolation as much as the common concern with George Willard that brings the collection together into a form of artistic unity that we can call a novel. What appears at first glance simply a collection of sketches begins to fall into a pattern when it is noticed that the last two sketches, "Sophistication" and "Departure," bring first the discussion of the problem of isolation to a conclusion, and then in two steps the story of George Willard to a conclusion. The earlier sketches had established the mind and character

of George as well as the added relevance of his mother's
hopes and fears for him; the reader knows at the end just
what it is that George is escaping from, or at least trying to
escape from. So, too, the earlier sketches had provided
glimpses of various kinds of human isolation and various attempts to meet it; the reader can understand only at the
end Anderson's final thoughts on the problem, dimly sensed
by George.

In that next-to-last sketch called "Sophistication" George
succeeds at last in establishing a momentary flash of understanding with Helen White, the girl with whom he is half in
love. When he finds her alone, apart at last from her family
and from a new suitor, he knows that there is some deeper
relationship here than he had previously known. "The feeling of loneliness and isolation that had come to the young
man in the crowded streets of his town was both broken and
intensified by the presence of Helen." [294] As they stand
together in the empty fair grounds they are increasingly
conscious of the two of them together in the midst of loneliness, conscious of some mutual understanding and love in
the face of the world. The intensity of the mood does not
last long, and they are soon on the way home again, but for a
moment they had held "the thing that makes the mature life
of men and women in the modern world possible." [298]
George, now just before leaving Winesburg, has slowly been
discovering just what this thing is, and it has been bound to
his new sense of maturity:

The eighteen years he has lived seem but a moment, a breathing
space in the long march of humanity. Already he hears death
calling. With all his heart he wants to come close to some other
human, touch someone with his hands, be touched by the hand
of another. If he prefers that the other be a woman, that is because he believes that a woman will be gentle, that she will understand. He wants, most of all, understanding. [287]

It is understanding, then, that makes life possible, that reaches
across the wall between lonely people and brings them into
some kind of sympathetic relationship. It is understanding
that defeats the isolation that tortures man.

The understanding that George finds as the solution to
the terrible problem of human isolation, however, seems more
nearly intuitive than rational. It is a flash of mutual comprehension that approaches love, an intuitive sympathetic vibra-
tion with the feelings of another that lifts both out of the
solitary heart. As such it is a fact rather than a solution.
George has always given sympathy to the revelations of the
lonely people about him and has given what understanding
he can. As far as this goes it is admirable and it is desirable.
It is at least headed in the right direction. But it is only with
Helen White that he finds, without seeking it, understanding
in its full meaning. There is no religious rationale here
and no philosophical one either. There is simply the growing
comprehension of the fact that intuitive understanding denies
loneliness and isolation. But the argument simply goes around
in a circle: where there is understanding there is no loneliness,
and in order to have understanding there must be no isolation
between two persons. It is a self-evident fact. And insofar
as it is a solution at all it is one that cannot be actively sought
and one that cannot be fought for, particularly within the
mind of the one who is himself lonely. Perhaps it is a realization of the hopelessness of the fact that makes *Winesburg,
Ohio* such a disturbing and even such a depressing book.
Anderson has no final and valid answer beyond sympathy for
the lonely people of his imagination.

It is a failure of understanding, of course, even in its more
restricted meaning, that creates the hopeless pathos aroused
by so many of the sketches. In some it is a failure of communication, of the ability of the lonely person to make others
even begin to understand what he means and what he feels.

The first sketch, in fact, the story of Wing Biddlebaum, called "Hands," begins the book with this central problem. As a former schoolteacher Wing had been unable to communicate in any deep sense with his pupils by words, but he had been able somehow to express himself with his hands. "He was one of those men in whom the force that creates life is diffused, not centralized. Under the caress of his hands doubt and disbelief went out of the minds of the boys and they began also to dream." [14] Inevitable tragedy followed, and he was soon accused of unspeakable things. Now he is a lonely and isolated man living out his life in Winesburg, fearful of his hands, and longing to express again his love of man. But love is no comfort in this world unless it is understood.

Kate Swift in "The Teacher" finds the same truth. She has a passionate desire to teach her former student George Willard to grasp the meaning of life and to interpret it honestly in his writing; and the wish has become entangled with passion itself, for she is a lonely young woman approaching the state of the old maid. But he can never fully understand her and can never see the relationship between the two sorts of passion. The result for her can only be lonely frustration and despair, for George as an everyday boy cannot follow her plea: " 'The thing to learn is to know what people are thinking about, not what they say.' " [192] There is no failure in her feeling toward him, there is failure only in her ability to make him understand it.

If understanding cannot be found between humans except in rare intuitive moments, some greater understanding transcending the merely human is desperately needed. But religion, the answer to isolation for so many of the great novels of the previous century, has no real meaning in Winesburg. In the series of three related sketches called "Godliness," "Surrender," and "Terror" religion is simply fanaticism that drives

men from society and hurts and destroys the family. In "The
Strength of God" it is a source of frustration, denying the
natural passions and turning the Reverend Curtis Hartman
into a guilty peeping Tom. Even his final renewal of faith
is an ironic one, based on misinterpretation and misunderstanding of the lonely plight of Kate Swift. Perhaps ordinary
human love would be a lesser answer, but there is no love
in Winesburg. George Willard takes Louise Trunnion out
into the night in "Nobody Knows," but it is just a casual
adventure for him, and the only beauty of the affair is that
nobody knows of it. Wash Williams' wife in "Respectability"
acquires three lovers in the first two years of marriage, and
Ray Pearson in "The Untold Lie" cannot honestly tell his
friend whether it is better to marry or not. The ordinary
concept of love leading to marriage and family and mutual
trust and affection is a lie for Winesburg, leading men and
women into betrayal and pain and greater isolation. Only
love that is the momentary flash of mutual understanding can
be the answer and the solution. But that love is not love in
its usual sense; it cannot be held; it cannot command loyalty
or faith; it bears nothing, believes nothing, hopes nothing.
In the moment of understanding that George Willard and
Helen White find, the boy rejects the sort of love that leads
to marriage or even to passion, for "he did not want at the
moment to be confused by her womanhood." [296] Man
cannot seek the solution or pray for it or devote himself and
his humanity to it; he can only hope—and in the world of
Winesburg, Ohio, it probably will not come.

The only antidote to loneliness that man can take for
himself is escape. If things become unendurable, the sketches
seem to say, then go somewhere else. The book ends, of
course, with George Willard leaving Winesburg for some
big city. Just what he expects to find there is not clear.
Other people in the various sketches have run away from

the past: Wing Biddlebaum left Pennsylvania in disgrace; Wash Williams ran away from Columbus hating women; Tom Foster and his grandmother left Cincinnati hoping for a better life. But none of them has succeeded in escaping from himself. The implication of the book is that George is escaping the narrow life and the circumscribing pettiness of the small town—*Winesburg, Ohio* does belong to that literary movement in revolt against the village. His final decision must be seen against the almost pathetic hope of his mother that he will not let himself be trapped in the stultifying atmosphere of Winesburg as she has been. She was a lonely woman, married to the shabby keeper of a small, shabby hotel, and the one remaining passion that gave her strength was the hope that George would escape just such a lonely, petty life. She herself in her last years had found some measure of solace in the half-understanding that she and Dr. Reefy had found, but that was only temporary. Her only final solution was death, the last escape from life. And now George at the end of the book is escaping from Winesburg, but one suspects that the escape is for him, too, only a temporary one. Death would seem the only really complete escape from life, but death is too final an answer. In the problem of isolation it, too, is simply a fact.

In the sketch that opens the collection and provides a sort of foreword and fictional frame, Anderson, speaking through the old writer, calls his characters "grotesques." In a sense, although perhaps not quite the one he meant, his description is fitting. Most of the people in the sketches are grotesque. They are twisted and abnormal, at odds with the world around them, somehow always limited and partial. A few are amusing, but most are pathetic. None is complete, none is wholly admirable, certainly none is heroic. There seems nothing left for the reader but pity and an occasional sympathetic shudder. In keeping, the impression left by their lonely, unhappy isolation is much the same. There is no solution for which they can try; they can only run away and hope for a momentary flash of understanding, knowing that death alone can finally solve their pathetic problem. There is no struggle against their fate, no heroic attempt to fight back, no consuming hope or faith. They can call only for pity, and at worst fall into a sort of self-pity for themselves and for mankind. There is little even approaching the tragic in their lot—only the pathos of the grotesque and the defeated and the hopeless. For Sherwood Anderson at least, man has ceased to be a potentially heroic creature, isolated and lonely but still at best willing to fight against the world or against himself. He is now only a grotesque to be analyzed, to be understood, to be pitied. Twentieth century man has arrived in fiction.

Understanding, escape, death, these are the consummations devoutly to be wished in the human isolation of Winesburg, Ohio—and with no fear or hope of the life to come, for it could be no worse than this life. And in this lonely life there are no final answers, there are no final truths about the isolated heart. In introducing his characters as grotesques Anderson presents his old writer thinking of the hundreds of different truths of life:

It was the truths that made the people grotesques. The old man had quite an elaborate theory concerning the matter. It was his notion that the moment one of the people took one of the truths to himself, called it his truth, and tried to live his life by it, he became a grotesque and the truth he embraced became a falsehood. [5]

To what extent his idea explains the characters of the sketches is debatable, but it does indicate the marked shift of the book from the novels of the preceding century. There in the great novels there were certain truths about isolation that could be accepted and held—and that did not turn the holder into a grotesque. There were challenging truths that brought out the best or the worst in a man, truths that could make Hester Prynne a heroine or Gilbert Osmond a loathsome object, but never truths that so canceled out each other that man was left in a lonely world without an ultimate truth to cling to. Man was then a being with enormous potential for good and evil, for suffering and for victory, for comedy and for tragedy. He was never simply a pathetic object to be analyzed and understood and pitied, although analysis and understanding and pity were as valid then as now. It is in this view of man as a pitiful grotesque that *Winesburg, Ohio* brings in the new century, not simply in its more direct interest in the inner life of the grotesque and the commonplace. The isolation of man with his lonely mind remains the same in these sketches, for that is a threat to all men. But the view of that state may change with time, and the only enduring answer to isolation that man has found may sometimes be forgotten or undiscovered or rejected, for that is the way of individual men, and individual novelists too.

Anderson may have rejected an answer, a truth, to isolation, but not all of the later novelists who took from him his interest in the grotesque within the commonplace joined him in his rejection. Certainly the characters in William Faulkner's *Light in August* are similar to Anderson's grotesques in their hint of abnormality and in their warped lives and thoughts, yet Faulkner's thematic conclusion is quite different from Anderson's. It is fitting that it should be, for even though Faulkner's novel follows logically from the novels of Anderson, and behind him Howells, it is a novel with its own strength that belongs not merely to the modern tradition but to the entire long tradition of the American novel. In some ways it has as much in common with Haw-

thorne and Twain and James as it does with the writing
of the novelists around Faulkner or immediately preceding
him. And certainly his theme of human isolation and his final
answer to this great problem of American life belongs to
other ages as well as to this one.

In keeping with Faulkner's now familiar fictional technique
of presenting his themes in almost symbolic fashion, *Light in
August* is a study of the human mind in exaggerated terms.
Unlike the earlier realism of Howells, Faulkner's novel
presents a group of characters who in situation and in action
are far beyond the "commonplace," although so successfully
set in a commonplace background and so surrounded by
commonplace details of the sort Howells advocated that
their relation to the familiar world of the reader would be
clear even if the symbolic meaning of character and action
were not. The characters are more nearly like Anderson's
grotesques, although often they are not so much grotesque as
they are simply exaggerated, in a manner not so very different
from the manner of Cooper and James. The reader recognizes
in them familiar problems and familiar responses enlarged
to the point of the unfamiliar. The effect is as though the
characters were placed under a microscope and enlarged far
beyond believable size, yet remain recognizable as the en-
largement of something believable and even commonplace.
The comparison to a subject under the microscope is apt too,
for, like Anderson, Faulkner gives the impression of presenting a group of interrelated "cases," of people who provide an
example and illustrate a point about human nature and the
human situation. Yet Faulkner's view of his characters seems
a more sympathetic one than Anderson's—his people are not
merely psychological cases—even though he retains sufficient
detachment to use his characters to make a thematic point.
In a fashion even reminiscent of Hawthorne, they are individual human beings of this century facing the problems of

human isolation, but they are also the human beings of any century in a series of symbolic situations.

Even a cursory survey of the characters of the novel will show the exaggeration. Joe Christmas, one of the central characters, is part Negro and part white, isolated from both races and unable to find his place in either world. He is finally killed and brutally mutilated in what amounts to a lynching with a thin cover of legality. The Reverend Gail Hightower is a former minister driven from his church by his congregation and lost to his faith. He lives imaginatively in the memory of the heroic military past of his grandfather, trying desperately to maintain a detachment from the life around him. Joanna Burden is a lonely spinster who tries to live in the South the life of a New England reformer of the past but finally surrenders to complete sensual abandon with Joe Christmas. She is brutally murdered. Even minor characters are grotesque and exaggerated. Doc Hines, Joe Christmas' grandfather, is a religious fanatic lost in an Old Testament concept of retributive justice, and in his madness thinking of himself as the agent of some grotesque Old Testament God. McEachern, the man who adopts Joe Christmas as a child, is so unrelenting in his religious faith, so hard and ruthlessly just, so scornful of the world of man, that he has never known pity or doubt. He too is murdered by Joe Christmas. All are lost people, isolated from life and from the world, terrible in their lonely lives as well as in their deaths. Only Byron Bunch and Lena Grove are capable of falling in love, of being at peace with themselves and with the world, and they provide a welcome interlude of normality and of loss of loneliness. But even they seem only to point up by contrast the isolation and the horror of the others. This is no fictional world of the commonplace or even of unhappy people in a quiet life, but a world of grotesque exaggeration in which man's familiar isolation is enlarged to the point of symbolic horror.

Joe Christmas is introduced in the story with a description that is to prove delicate and accurate:

There was something definitely rootless about him, as though no town nor city was his, no street, no walls, no square of earth his home. And that he carried his knowledge with him always as though it were a banner, with a quality ruthless, lonely, and almost proud. [27] [3]

He is without family, without friends, without home, without race. Half Negro and half white, he has grown up first in an orphanage, then in an adopted home without love or understanding, and finally in the open streets of the land. In childhood he had been pursued by the hatred of a fanatical grandfather bent on punishing him for his Negro blood. As a youth he had been treated with a brutal, rigorous fairness by the puritanical McEachern (varied by the weak softness of Mrs. McEachern), until his own humanity drove him into flight. Then came that long period undescribed in the novel when he wandered the land, alternately driven by his Negro blood and his white blood, unable to accept either, unable to commit himself to one race or the other. Even in Jefferson, where his final days are played out, he never really belongs. He takes a menial Negro job at the mill, although never with permanence, and he lives in the Negro cabin behind Miss Burden's house. But he will never admit publicly his Negro blood, and turns down with scorn Miss Burden's plea that he go to a Negro college and become a Negro lawyer. He engages in a sensual orgy with Miss Burden, but his motivation is not so much passion or desire as the need to subdue her with the physical fact of his Negro blood. From the moment of birth to the moment of death he is an outcast, isolated from the world around him

[3] Page references are to William Faulkner, *Light in August* (New York: Harrison Smith and Robert Haas, 1932). My thanks for copyright permission go to Random House, Inc.

by his nature and by his past. He is human isolation taken to its ultimate point.

In his final confused flight from the law after his murder of Joanna Burden he escapes neither the pursuit nor himself; he is still inside the circle of isolation in which he has always lived:

"And yet I have been further in these seven days than in all the thirty years," he thinks. "But I have never got outside that circle. I have never broken out of the ring of what I have already done and cannot ever undo," he thinks quietly. [321]

And there can be no escape for him. The past is an arbiter of the present for him as for the others in this novel, and there is no escape from it. His past is made up of his own actions—the flights, the murders, the fight with the world and with himself—but it is also made up of the mere facts of his birth and his childhood, the volitionless facts that led to the voluntary acts. From the beginning he was shoved forward against his will, or rather without regard to his will, on the road that led inevitably to his isolation and his suffering and his violent death. Yet, being human, he tries to resist the idea that he is, after all, only a victim of some impersonal fate over which he has no control. As his life nears its end he sits one August night in Miss Burden's ruined garden with a momentary understanding: "He believed with calm paradox that he was the volitionless servant of the fatality in which he believed that he did not believe." [264] He cannot believe in fate, for that would destroy his pride in himself, yet he cannot not believe in fate, for that would deny the life he has lived. In his introspection, as in his life itself, he is caught in the isolated circle that always leads back to where it began.

The pride of Joe Christmas is an element that must be taken into account. With nothing outside in which to take pride, nothing to which he can belong with self-respect, he must turn within for pride and respect. And the very pride makes his situation worse. In self-protection he can give nothing of himself to others, and he remains an isolated man, "a spirit, strayed out of its own world, and lost." [106] In his past there had been no love lost on him, and now he neither expects love nor gives it. Men such as his boot-legging companion Joe Brown are to be used without asking or giving affection or respect—and with men like Brown it is the only possible course. Women may be used for diversion or even for support but never given love. A woman like Joanna Burden may even be used to further pride in self, at least until she tries to force him to accept the humility of his Negro blood. But he knows from the past that he must never surrender anything of himself to a woman. If he does, eventually she will either curse him as Bobbie Allen the little prostitute had done when he fell in love as a boy, or she will try to capture his lonely spirit by a too soft and cloying sweetness as Mrs. McEachern had tried.

Similarly, he can commit himself wholly to neither black nor white. If he accepts his Negro blood, he is forced into the involuntary humility of the Negro; if he tries to pass as white, which the community has made for him a matter of pride, he is sooner or later found out. The only escape from the dilemma that he can find is to withdraw even further into himself, cultivate so far as possible his own pride and self-respect, and snarl at the world outside. It is no wonder that a mute, sullen, impotent rage is the impression that he presents to the world.

In contrast to the mute rage of Joe Christmas the equally mute detachment from the outer world of the Reverend Gail Hightower shows even more clearly. He too is isolated from the world, but, unlike Joe Christmas, he enjoys his state of isolation and carefully cultivates it. He even thinks of himself as dead to the world: " 'I am not in life any more,' he thinks. 'That's why there is no use in even trying to meddle, interfere.' " [284] He lives only in the memory of the past— for he too is controlled by the past—and in imagination gallops in the brave, foolhardy, glorious raid of his grandfather on the Union depot at Jefferson during the Civil War. He had once made a specious attempt to join the modern world, had studied at a seminary, married, taken a church. But the church was carefully chosen at Jefferson, and the wife was chosen only because it was the thing to do—and, besides, she could help get the church at Jefferson. His neglected wife, to him a mere shade who could not match in brilliance or attraction the shades of that Confederate cavalry, had soon gone off to lead her own life and in the ensuing scandal to cost him his church. Hightower had been secretly delighted—it even showed in the photograph of him being driven from the church—and settled down after the flurry of indignation of the town in the quiet isolation of Jefferson to grow obese and contented, living only in those glorious visions of the past. His habitual expression is one of denial and flight, for he feels that he has earned his detachment and his freedom from mankind: " 'I have bought immunity. I have paid. I have paid.' " [292] Now he is a lonely man who does not even feel that he belongs to the world of man, and he can listen to the problems of others as from a distance: "It is as though he were listening to the doings of people of a different race." [74] Like Joe Christmas, he is alone and exists only for himself; all others are of a different race.

But Hightower wants to keep it that way. Or at least he thinks he does. Sitting alone in his house dreaming of the past, he believes that he has dissociated himself from mankind. But even before the final pressure that forces him back into life again there are indications that his detach-

ment is held only by effort and will, not simply by easy
inclination. There is, for instance, the occasion when some
four years before the present time in the novel Hightower
had broken from his isolation to deliver a Negro baby. And
now when he first hears that Joe Christmas has Negro blood,
his immediate response is one of fear and pity: " 'Think,
Byron; what it will mean when the people—if they catch . . .
Poor man. Poor mankind.' " [93] But it is when Byron
Bunch begins to force him into participation in the tragic
situation of Joe Christmas that his reasoned desire for detachment, his belief that he has bought immunity from the
involvements and pains of life, comes into real conflict with
his instinctive pity for mankind, a pity amounting almost
to moral responsibility. The struggle is so great that it shows
even in the physical body:

He is shaking, steadily; he looks up now. In the lamplight his
face looks slick, as if it had been oiled. Wrung and twisted, it
gleams in the lamplight; the yellowed, oftwashed shirt which was
fresh this morning is damp with sweat. "It's not because I cant,
dont dare to," he says; "it's because I wont! I wont! do you
hear?" . . . Byron does not move. . . . *It aint me he is shouting
at. It's like he knows there is something nearer him than me to
convince of that.* [370]

Like Huck Finn, he is caught between the desire for isolation and an instinctive sense of participation, and the dilemma
can be resolved only after a bitter struggle with himself,
and only by firmly committing himself to one side or the
other.

Joe Christmas almost literally cannot commit himself, but
the Reverend Gail Hightower can if he will. Here, then,
is the central thematic contrast of the novel, the point to
which all else in the novel leads. Ironically, each man thinks
of his isolation in a half-truth, unwilling to face the fact
of the responsibility for his plight. Joe Christmas senses

that he is isolated by an impersonal fate, a source and a past over which he has had no control, but to preserve his pride and his self-respect he must believe that he is what he is by deliberate choice. Hightower, on the other hand, to preserve his self-respect in the face of his instinctive sense of moral responsibility must believe that his isolation has been forced on him by an impersonal fate and the accidents of his past. Yet he senses that his situation is the result of deliberate choice, and knows it when Byron Bunch tells him so directly. After hearing of the plight of Joe Christmas and the others, he says to Byron Bunch that he is no longer a man of God, and through no choice of his own. But Byron answers: " 'You were given your choice before I was born, and you took it before I or her or him either was born. That was your choice. And I reckon them that are good must suffer for it the same as them that are bad.' " [345] Hightower is what he is through choice, not through destiny, and he must eventually determine his life through choice.

Hightower had first chosen the way of a man of God, even if the choice was casual and his career mingled inextricably with bright dreams of the heroic past. Then when he was cast out of his church, and even before, he seemed to forget the way. At best the church seemed another dream of the past, except for those evenings when in imagination he follows the service and feels again the peace of the church:

Then alone . . . is there something of that peace which is the promise and the end of the Church. The mind and the heart purged then, if it is ever to be; . . . the heart quiet now for a little while beneath the cool soft blowing of faith and hope. [346–47]

But faith and hope are always there too, even when denied, and are as powerful in his final choice as his desire for isolation from the troubles of man. For a long time that

peace is only a memory for Hightower or a vicarious emotional experience to be sensed from a distance. But by the
final moment of choice he has learned that the peace must
be earned, must be fought for against his inner desire for
isolation and for lack of commitment to man or God. However much he may try to deny it, he knows that this peace
must be deliberately chosen and paid for, just as he tries
to believe that he has paid for his immunity from life. And,
unlike Joe Christmas, he knows it can be chosen and can be
found. One of the lurid and exaggerated flashes of Joe
Christmas' final flight is that of his standing in the pulpit
of a Negro church, surrounded by his own violence, cursing
God. There is no peace for Joe Christmas; at best his is
only a wistful, passing thought, "thinking *God perhaps and
me not knowing that too* He could see it like a printed
sentence, fullborn and already dead *God loves me too* like
the faded and weathered letters on a last year's billboard
God loves me too." [98]. But for Hightower it can be more
than a wistful thought if he will only throw away the
apparent peace of detachment that is its delusive substitute.
And his agony is that he knows it.

In the end he chooses the peace of God, and the contrast
to the violent, lonely, tortured life of Joe Christmas is complete. The outward gestures, the surface commitments do not
seem great. At the prompting of Byron Bunch from without
and his own sympathy from within he helps the unwed Lena
Grove bear her baby. The very exposure to new life and to
the almost comic involvements of Brown, the father who does
not love Lena, and Byron, the outsider who does love her,
seems to return Hightower to life and to humanity again.
Then at the last minute, driven by the immediacy of the
moment as well as by the moral commitment that he has
been trying to deny all of his life, he gasps out the lie to
Joe Christmas' pursuers that Christmas had been with him

on the night of the murder. They ignore him, of course, and his gesture has no outward result. Ironically, Grimm, the fanatic pursuer who likes to believe that he is simply a representative of the impersonal law of the land, answers Hightower with an oath, " 'Jesus Christ!' " [439] But the inner result in Hightower is transforming. Or perhaps better, the gesture is a sign of a growing inner transformation. From that moment Hightower is a changed man, and the climax of his story is his growing realization, reluctant but irresistible, of the degree to which he has strayed from the path of the man of God. Joe Christmas' turning almost instinctively to Hightower's house for a sanctuary is more nearly prophetic than he could know.

The climax of Hightower's transformation comes after the death of Joe Christmas and the birth of Lena Grove's child. Upon his return from Lena he had felt something of pride in his deed and in his return to the life of man: "a glow, a wave, a surge of something almost hot, almost triumphant. 'I showed them!' he thinks. 'Life comes to the old man yet.' " [382–83] But this is only a step along the way. The climax comes as he sits at his window in the dusk looking back over his life just as it had come to Isabel Archer as she sat one night looking back over her life. Faulkner's sustained image of Hightower's thought is of the wheel of some vehicle turning in sand. It is a good image, for it suggests the slow, painful revolving of his thought dragging itself inch by inch through a clinging and retarding medium, driven by some enormous power. And now as he comes to the end of his thoughts he painfully recognizes the tragic error of his life. He sees that it was he who was the instrument of his wife's despair and death rather than she who was responsible for his isolation. But this recognition is simply a corollary of his final acceptance of the fact that what he has been was his own deliberate choice: "He seems to watch himself, alert, patient, skillful, playing his cards well, making it appear that he was being driven, uncomplaining, into that which he did not even then admit had been his desire since before he entered the seminary." [463] Byron Bunch had told him this before, but he could never quite accept the fact. Now he finds it for himself and accepts it, and at last he is a free man recognizing the implications of the free will that he would never before admit. And for him, coming so late, the recognition has all of the terror of Joe Christmas' very lack of free will.

His life has always been bound to the church, either in acceptance or rejection. And now as full summation of his recognition of the truth of his life he sees what a false role he has been playing. The church itself, "skypointed not with ecstasy or passion but in adjuration, threat, and doom" [461], is not what it should be, but that is in part his fault, for he had accepted and served the church as it is, and had even used it to forward his own desires. He had failed the real promise of the church and the potentiality of his ministry, no matter what others in the church might also have been doing. As he sits quietly in his window he seems to see his own face in the pulpit mirrored in the face of the con-gregation—and leading them astray just as he was leading himself astray.

He seems to see reflected in them a figure antic as a showman, a little wild: a charlatan preaching worse than heresy, in utter dis-regard of that whose very stage he preempted, offering instead of the crucified shape of pity and love, a swaggering and un-chastened bravo. [462]

Here is the full horror of his isolation, for it had not only separated him from man but from God. And what is worse, because of his original voluntary choice of the ministry and of the detachment of isolation—a simultaneous choice that he sees now as an invalid and even wicked paradox—he has failed to lead others to the peace of God that is the only real immunity. He has failed himself, he has failed others, and he has failed God.

With the inner recognition of his spiritual state and the outer action to atone for his state and even destroy it, Hightower has at last approached that peace that he so longs for.

In the lambent suspension of August into which night is about to fully come, it seems to engender and surround itself with a faint glow like a halo. The halo is full of faces. The faces are not shaped with suffering, not shaped with anything: not horror, pain, not even reproach. They are peaceful, as though they have escaped into an apotheosis; his own is among them. [465]

It is the end of his life, the goal and the reward; now he has the triumph and the desire, the full life and the glory, to match that other triumph and that other glory of the galloping ghosts of the past, now at last to leave his mind in peace. Through his own agonizing thought, aided only by his moral and religious instincts and the force of passing circumstance, he has found that peace he had sought for so long in isolation. Whether he has literally come to the end of his life is left in ambiguity, for it is not important. Only Joe Christmas had to die to end his terrible isolation and find his peace. Perhaps it is here, in his isolated, sacrificial death, that the implication of his name "Christmas," at once so fitting and so ironically and completely wrong, shows its relevance. Both men leave the same final impression: musing, quiet, steadfast, serene, triumphant. And that is as it should be, for both men have reached the only possible end to the agony of their lonely isolation.

In the story of these two men, so different and yet with so much in common, the novel finds its thematic center.

Other characters move through the novel and have their own importance, but an importance always subordinated to these two. Only Lena Grove and Byron Bunch might seem of equal interest, and they in fact reinforce the central theme. Lena Grove might have been an outcast like Joe Christmas, but her natural lack of self-consciousness and her sense of belonging fully to the earth, qualities not so very unlike those of Ántonia Shimerda, draw the sympathies of others to her and prevent it. Her often reiterated " 'It was right kind of you all' " [20] is almost a motif for her. Byron Bunch, the lonely conscientious, silent man, might have withdrawn into the isolation of a Hightower, but his sensitivity to others and his immediate ability to feel love and sympathy prevent it. Only these two are not warped into grotesques by their past, and it is fitting that at the end of the novel they are drifting toward marriage. They do not have to fight themselves or their world as Hightower and Joe Christmas do. They are the unisolated of this life who make the plight of the others even sharper by contrast.

Only Hightower and Joe Christmas are at the real center, and their story points out how solidly *Light in August* is set in the tradition of American fiction. It is unmistakably a novel of this century; the element of the grotesque and the immediate interest in the inner mind are representative. Joe Christmas seems particularly to fit this pattern. But the novel also belongs in another sense to the inherited pattern. In coming to grips with the problem of human isolation it is in the great American tradition. And its solution to the problem, illustrated in the story of Hightower, is the traditional solution. The only final and completely satisfying answer is the one discovered by Hester Prynne and Isabel Archer and even Huck Finn: the loss of self in love or sympathy or concern for others. At its source is what Hightower calls and learns to recognize as "the crucified shape of pity and love."

Light in August, like *The Scarlet Letter,* finds this answer in direct religious terms, as is particularly fitting, where other novels used other terms. But whatever the terms, the answer remains the same: to escape from the isolation of the self man must deny the self.

The answer is the traditional one, but the novel, in keeping with its setting in the modern world, asks a question that the modern world seems to pose. Hightower finds his answer —the answer—but what of Joe Christmas, whose isolation is the result of a past and a present, an impersonal and ir- resistible situation, over which he has no control and against which he can exert no force? The traditional answer is depend- ent upon the existence of free will in man, but what if there is no free will? This is the question that the modern age has thrust at man, the question that Sherwood Anderson asks so forcibly, and Joe Christmas is Faulkner's dramatic example of it. The churchman, like Howells in the novel of this ordinary world, would probably insist still upon the answer found by Hightower, saying there is no possibility in man of the absence of free will. Even Joe Christmas seems at times obscurely to sense this concept—and to preserve his self- respect tries to believe it. But in this novel Faulkner, like Anderson, would not seem to be so sure, and the only answer offered for Joe Christmas is violent death. In these two men, the Reverend Gail Hightower and Joe Christmas, the old answer and the new question meet, and the resolution is painful and difficult.

Perhaps the meeting of the old answer and a new question is a mark of any step forward in the traditional theme of isolation in the novel. If so, John Steinbeck's *The Grapes of Wrath* marked another such step for the modern age when it took up the question of isolation not only for a few par- ticular characters but for a whole people, and considered it in a novel that belongs in many respects with *The Rise of Silas*

Lapham and *Winesburg, Ohio* in a group of the grotesque and
the commonplace. It is a novel of the agricultural depression
of the 1930's and that memory of the folly and failure of
man, the dust bowl. Yet it is a novel not about conditions but
about people, the commonplace people of a Howells—even
though Howells would have been shocked at the novel
itself. Steinbeck's despair and indignation are too great for
a Howells, and his characters are far from the familiar society
of a Howells. Like Anderson and Faulkner, in contrast to
Howells, he even questions the assumption of free will in
the individual. Yet his people must meet the commonplace
problems of life—food, shelter, clothing, medical aid—and their
desires are the desires of the commonplace man—happiness,
love, family unity, self-respect, a feeling of belonging. They
are the common men of the new century. In another sense,
however, the novel is not about commonplace man but about
a special, often grotesque group of men, the Okies, the
dispossessed of the dust bowl, the new itinerant farm laborers
of California. And one of the successes of the novel is the
manner in which it conveys simultaneously the impression,
almost an epic impression, of a whole people migrating
westward and the familiar view of one particular family
facing its particular problems. The Joad family, even though
unique, is a part of a whole people; and this novel, unlike
most of the novels of the previous century, is as much about
a people as it is about a few central people. In the midst of a
blighting depression the concern for the individual begins
to give way to the concern for the people, even though
paradoxically it was this novel, probably more than any
other, that convinced America that the group scornfully
called Okies was after all made up of familiar and commonplace individuals.

There are isolated and lonely and even grotesque individuals
in the novel. Uncle John, the "lonest goddamn man in the

world,' " [94] [4] who let his wife die of appendicitis, thinking
it only a stomach ache, is forever after lost in his sense of
guilt, a marked and isolated man in his own mind. Casy,
the former preacher who has lost his old faith, is a lonely
man looking for some new faith. And Muley Graves, who
stays behind in Oklahoma, is only a lonely ghost haunting
an empty land:

"I'd tell myself, 'I'm lookin' after things so when all the folks
come back it'll be all right.' But I knowed that wan't true. There
ain't nothin' to look after. The folks ain't never comin' back.
I'm jus' wanderin' aroun' like a damn ol' graveyard ghos'." [69]

But Casy and Muley are parts of a larger pattern, the isolation
of a people. Casy is to be their spokesman, finally to give
words to their deepest feeling, and Muley is a result of the
people's migration and a sign of their departure. For the central
isolation of the novel is that of a whole people. Driven from
home and land, they have lost the sense of belonging: " 'Place
where folks live is them folks. They ain't whole, out lonely
on the road in a piled-up car. They ain't alive no more.' "
[71] At home they had been a part of the land, had belonged
to it and had felt their roots go down. Then came the drought
and the banks and the tractors, and suddenly there was a
home no longer, there was no place to belong to. And without
a country there is only lonely wandering. The young and the
strong can bear the isolation, but for the old, too long
rooted, it is like leaving life itself. Grampa dies before they
can even carry him out of the state.

The people have lost their old home and cannot find a new
one. No one somewhere else wants them to belong; no one
wants them at all. On the migration west, California shines
ahead as a newer and greener home. But along the way,
prophetically, they are met only with hatred and suspicion

[4] Page references are to John Steinbeck, *The Grapes of Wrath* (New
York: The Viking Press, 1939).

and contempt, tempered occasionally with a touch of human pity. California does not even have the pity. On first arrival at the California line a fellow Okie had offered the Joads a warning not believed then but soon to prove too true:

"People gonna have a look in their eye. They gonna look at you an' their face says, 'I don't like you, you son-of-a-bitch.' Gonna be deputy sheriffs, an' they'll push you aroun'. You camp on the roadside, an' they'll move you on. You gonna see in people's face how they hate you." [280]

There the people are scared for fear their country in turn will be taken from them by this new horde of hungry and landless and homeless, and they try to drive them away by fair means or foul. The Californians are willing to use them for gain, to demand the greatest work for the least pay, knowing the hungry cannot refuse, but never to offer them permanence or a home, never a country of their own. The Joads and their kind, the new migratory people are as isolated from this country as from their own far behind, unable to live there, unwanted here. If they settle for a moment, they are soon driven off by hunger or by pick handles. And if they complain or protest, they are reds or agitators or dangerous vagrants, and the police and the mobs are eager for violence. There is no immediate solution—whatever history with its slow movement may later have provided—and the lonely people seem destined to wander forever in isolation. It is fitting that the novel ends with the Joads wiser and more experienced, but still with no sense of belonging, no permanence in the country, no home of their own.

With no sense of belonging to anything outside, the people must turn within their own group for comfort and strength and loss of loneliness. The family is the all-important unit, as it was in *My Antonia*, as it must be when there is nothing else to which to belong with any meaning. Before the migration the Joad family had been scattered about their region, but it comes together for the great trek, and its unity is a large part of its strength. Ma, at the center of the family, soon becomes the accepted leader and the source of unity and confidence and will; and her one unvarying demand is for the family to stay together no matter what happens: " 'All we got is the family unbroke. Like a bunch a cows, when the lobos are ranging, stick all together. I ain't scared while we're all here, all that's alive, but I ain't gonna see us bust up.' " [231] And she is right. Like the Lapham family, although so different in surface and in circumstance, as long as the family is together there is no isolation for the individual member, whatever his weakness and his failure. Ma can be fierce in her determination, and she can even back up her demands with a jack handle when necessary, for she knows that the family is all that they have left to depend upon: " 'What we got lef' in the worl'? Nothin' but us. Nothin' but the folks.' " [230] But despite her wisdom and her determination the family unity does begin to crumble, and it is the nearest to a real defeat that the Joads ever reach. Grampa and Granma die along the way, Noah leaves the family at the California border, Connie abandons Rosasharn and the family, Tom is driven away by the sheriffs and by his conscience, and at the end of the story Al is about to leave with his new promised wife. Some of these losses are inevitable and unavoidable, others are the result of too great an individual weakness, but each tends to lessen the fierce family loyalty and will that carry the Joads through their trials and their loneliness. If the Joads are ever broken—and even in their reduced numbers it is hard to imagine—it will be because the family itself is broken. But affairs never reach that desperate a state and never will as long as Ma is there to hold the rest of the family together in defiance of the hostile world.

An awareness of the value and the comfort of the family

is not limited to the Joads, of course, but is an element of the entire migration. And under the pressures of a common need the whole people slowly become one large family in themselves. The Joads, the particular example, find themselves losing a few members of the real family but quickly picking up others who are accepted almost as real members. The family in the long run does not diminish but rather expands more and more. Preacher Casy had early been accepted as a member, and along the road Mr. and Mrs. Wilson are added until sickness forces them out again. Others move more quickly in and out. But these are simply examples of a continuous process in which all the people find themselves increasingly drawn into a larger family relationship. Camping along Route 66 headed west, the process begins: "In the evening a strange thing happened: the twenty families became one family, the children were the children of all. The loss of home became one loss, and the golden time in the West was one dream." [264]

In the West itself in the face of united hostility the process is even stronger, as it must be. Soon the world for the Joads is divided into "our kind of folks" or even just "our folks" and the hostile "them." And here the larger family must stand together if it is to stand at all, and the lesser family, the literal family, is just the starting point. Even Ma recognizes the new fact as she thanks the woman who had shared their temporary housing in a boxcar and helped with Rosasharn's delivery:

"You been frien'ly," she said. "We thank you."
The stout woman smiled. "No need to thank. Ever'body's in the same wagon. S'pose we was down. You'd a give us a han'."
"Yes," Ma said, "we would."
"Or anybody."
"Or anybody. Use' ta be the fambly was fust. It ain't so now. It's anybody. Worse off we get, the more we got to do." [606]

Among the Okies struggling to exist in an alien land the family of man is more than a sentimental phrase. It is a practical and a necessary fact of existence.

The family of man is more even than a necessity for the Joads: it is an ideal of the novel. At the lowest level it appears in a form familiar during the depression, the hopeful ideal of men working together in some form of unity to protect their economic and social rights. Only organized resistance of many can demand a fair wage, for instance, and the idea is illustrated in the strike led by Preacher Casy against the peach growers. When he is killed for his efforts he is a martyr to a worthy ideal, although most of the people do not even recognize the fact. Or when the migrants band together to run the camp at Weedpatch, a camp that is clean, decent, orderly, and without deputy sheriffs from outside, the people are beginning to move toward a social ideal. These are ideals that present themselves immediately to the people, for they are caught in a life-or-death struggle in which money and living conditions are of vital concern, and on the surface at least are the only concerns. But in the novel as a whole they are simply corollaries of a greater concern with the ideal of the family of man, of the moving, as Steinbeck puts it, from "I" to "we." [206] Here Preacher Casy is the spokesman for the ideal, stating it directly, and the one who attempts as well to live it, although he ends by dying for it.

When Casy first appears in the novel he is a troubled man who has lost his first sure faith, but, unlike the Reverend Gail Hightower, he has never lost the spirit of a faith or the sure desire of a faith. He is a lost and lonely man wandering in the wilderness to question his own mind and to define just what it is that he does believe. But whatever his doubts, he knows he still has a mission to perform: " 'Here I got the sperit sometimes an' nothin' to preach about. I got the call

to lead people, an' no place to lead 'em.' " [29] In the trek
to California he finds a place to lead the people, and along
the way he finds a faith to preach. The faith is a love of
people themselves and a belief in a total soul of humanity
and is participated in by all men, a commonality of man in
the sight of God that makes one man alone an incomplete
creature: " 'not one fella for another fella, but one fella
kind of harnessed to the whole shebang—that's right, that's
holy.' " [110] Then when his half-understood philosophy
is brought up against the injustice of the world his way
ahead is clear. His first chance to put his belief into dramatic
action comes when he offers himself to save Tom and a
friend from a bullying sheriff. His second comes when he
leads the strike against starvation pay in the peach orchard.
There he is killed by the representatives of a harsher and a
more selfish law. But his preaching will go on through the
lips of Tom Joad, who has inherited his belief and, thinking
back to Casy's words, can say, " 'But I know now a fella ain't
no good alone.' " [570] There is the central point of the
novel, and there is the conviction on which the overt social
protest of the novel is based.

Casy believes that his new faith is not Christianity, even
though he finds texts in *Ecclesiastes* to make his point.
Perhaps it is not, although in effect it reaches the same
belief in the brotherhood of man under the fatherhood of
God. Certainly it is not the hell-fire, damnation, washed-in-
the-blood, shout-to-the-Lamb religion that Casy and most of
his flock had known before. It is perhaps nearer to a moral
humanism with the Christian tradition behind it. But whatever it is, it teaches that a man cannot live by and for
himself alone. When early in the novel Tom Joad says,
" 'I'm just tryin' to get along without shovin' nobody
around,' " [13–14] he suggests, too, another paradoxical aspect of the same thought. For the novel seems divided into

those who are intent on hurting others and those who want
to avoid hurting others. The moral assumption is that a man
must lead his own life as best he can, and others must allow
him to if possible: " 'On'y one thing in this worl' I'm sure of,
an' that's I'm sure nobody got a right to mess with a fella's
life. He got to do it all hisself. Help him, maybe, but not tell
him what to do.' " [306] The only demand is that his life
must not hurt others. The common belief lying behind both
assumptions, the need for a feeling of the mutual ties of
humanity and the need for allowing a man to lead his life
unmolested, is the belief in the value of the individual life.
And both the cause and the result of this belief are the ideal
of love of humanity or the human spirit. Casy, in hesitantly
defining his beliefs, must inevitably work through the point:
" 'Maybe . . . it's all men an' all women we love; maybe
that's the Holy Sperit—the human sperit—the whole shebang.' " [32–33] The life of all humanity is holy, and so
must be the life of the individual within it. With the love of
others, the love of humanity given and taken, loneliness is
impossible, even in the midst of isolation. The trouble is
that not all men are so morally committed, and those who
are must often suffer isolation from the others.

In *The Grapes of Wrath* there are plenty of "others" to
hold the Okies in isolation. Sometimes they act out of the
brutality and hatred born of fear, as the deputies who destroy
the Hooverville camps. Sometimes they act out of selfishness
and desire for personal gain, as the orchard owners who
break up the strike against starvation wages. But whatever
the immediate motivation, all deny the humanity and the
individual worth of the Okies. The service-station boy on
Route 66, even though he takes no direct action, is representative in his thought:

"Well, you and me got sense. Them goddamn Okies got no sense
and no feeling. They ain't human. A human being wouldn't live

like they do. A human being couldn't stand it to be so dirty and miserable. They ain't a hell of a lot better than gorillas." [301] Against the isolation imposed by such an attitude the Okies see no recourse beyond banding together more solidly in mutual aid and understanding. If at times they believe too much in mere organization for its own sake—defended in part by the assumption of the common nature of man—their longing can be understood in terms of the times and their situation. The "others," after all, have banded together, not out of a desire to serve their common humanity, but rather out of a selfish desire to exploit the unorganized. For the individual to fight back alone may be heroic, but it is fatal. As an extreme case of the isolated individual against the world the story of Pretty Boy Floyd is mentioned again and again: " 'They run him like a coyote, an' him a-snappin' an' a-snarlin', mean as a lobo.' " [103] But the Okies of this novel do not turn into that sort of outlaw. Driven out of the home and the society they once knew, wandering in isolation among those who cannot even accept them as members of a common humanity, they can only turn to each other for help and understanding and love. And there, bound together by their mutual plight, forced into a recognition of the humanity of others, they can lose the loneliness that their isolation threatens.

For all its modern setting, then, for all its time of unusual conditions and its interest in a whole people as well as in the individual, *The Grapes of Wrath* is still clearly in the tradition of the American concern in fiction for the problem of isolation. It has simply broadened the theme, in keeping with the sociological interest imposed by the century, to include a group rather than a single person. The Joads must each meet the problem of alienation in his own way, yet behind the individual there is always the family, and behind the family there is always the whole tribe of migrants, each individual and each group of which must meet the problem too. And the answer for all is still the old answer for the individual: the loss of self in concern and love for others. If man can lose his exclusively egocentric and selfish interest to turn outward to others, he need not fear loneliness or spiritual isolation. For this century the mechanics of the solution may be somewhat different from those of earlier days. Man can no longer simply turn to humanity—desirable as that ideal is—but must belong to some form of group to which to turn. Even then the answer is not simple, for the group may itself be devoted to inhumane ends, as is the organization of farmers and canners in this novel. So man must turn to the group, and the group must turn to humanity itself. The individual is no longer in complete control of his own end, as Anderson and Faulkner imply, but must depend upon others as well as himself. But the others, as *The Grapes of Wrath* insists so successfully, are themselves individuals. And if the individuals of this modern complex, organized world would always keep faith with their common humanity in their necessary organization, the ideal world in which there is no isolation and no loneliness would be achieved. The goal may never be reached—and the fiction of this century is hardly optimistic—but man in the meanwhile has an immediate answer that will serve his needs and will eventually help the step toward the ideal. When man can turn out of himself to others he can escape spiritual loneliness, whatever his isolation may be.

With *The Grapes of Wrath* one method of presenting the theme of isolation reaches fulfillment, if not climax, making way undoubtedly for other methods to be slowly developed. When William Dean Howells began insisting that the novel must be realistic in presenting the commonplace of American life, he probably never imagined that realism would include the grotesque as well—in fact he would probably have said

that the two are contradictory—or that the commonplace in a
new age would be a matter of a whole people in despair as
well as of a few individuals concerned with the decencies of
daily life. Yet that is what happened, though literary historians
may want to trace the development along other and equally
satisfactory paths. The theme of isolation, however, remained
a constant, even though the method of presenting it and the
fictional situations in which it was dramatized varied as
American life varied to meet the new needs. And the majority
of novelists considering that new American life agreed that
the old and traditional answer to isolation, however difficult
or impossible it might be to attain, remained not only valid
but still the only valid answer. It had to answer new demands
of the warped and psychologically wounded, it had to meet
new doubts of the final free will of man, it even had to apply
to a whole helpless sociological group as well as to the strong
and independent individual, but it still met the demand. If
some novels were doubtful or skeptical, it was not so much of
the answer as of the possibility of accepting and living with
that answer. Isolation in the new America, it seemed, was
not really so different after all from isolation in the old.
The theme and its conclusion were too basic and too traditional in American life to alter even in the new and changing novel.

V

Conclusion:
The Monkey-Rope

The discussion of other individual novels could go on seemingly forever. As long as the American novel continues its concern with the theme of human isolation there will be no lack of examples or of variations on the theme, and the novel shows no signs at the moment of abandoning the concern. Two or three of the subjects that even the current best seller has made popular take up directly the question of isolation. The war novels in which the isolated individual is pitted against the impersonality of war and the army—James Jones's *From Here to Eternity* (1951), for instance, or Leon Uris' *Battle Cry* (1953)—offer their dramatization of the theme, sometimes with an almost raucous insistence. The popular novels of academic life, such as Mary McCarthy's *The Groves of Academe* (1952), are immediately relevant. Or the currently very popular novels of the conflicting demands of the individual and the business world, such as Sloan Wilson's *The Man in the Gray Flannel Suit* (1955) or Cameron Hawley's *Cash McCall* (1955), seem almost to serve as direct illustrations of the problems of individualism and conformity that so engross the American today. To go back to older novels, a good many others might be chosen, either by the same authors discussed here or by different authors. It would be interesting, for instance, to examine in some detail the handling of the theme in such an early novel as Hugh Henry Brackenridge's long, rambling story of the Pennsylvania frontier, *Modern Chivalry* (1792–1815). The lost generation of the first World War in Ernest Hemingway's *The Sun Also Rises* (1926) would certainly find its place in the historical theme. But there is no point in piling up possibilities; the problem for the critic and the historian is not in finding examples but in choosing among them.

The handful chosen here from among the best novels, however, are representative enough to allow a number of general conclusions about the theme of human isolation in the American novel. A few conclusions do not need stressing. Certainly the relationship of the theme itself to American life of the past and present, complex though that relationship may often be, is one that may be assumed without argument. It varies, of course, from novel to novel: Cooper's *Deerslayer* presents an idyllic picture of a life of romantic isolation written at a time when such a life was becoming more and more obviously impossible. Mark Twain, in turn, picks up in *Huckleberry Finn* something of Cooper's nostalgia but does not divorce it entirely from a realistic moral view of the life he sees around him. John Steinbeck in the twentieth century tries in *Grapes of Wrath* to present a believable account of the isolation of the very real life of his own time. There is no easy formula for relating any novel to its time, beyond the general statement that a novelist's assumptions, ideas, and beliefs are always conditioned, if not directly formed, by the time and the culture in which he lives. In turn, his expression of his ideas is directed toward his own time, whether in agreement or disagreement, praise or protest. Looking back with all the luxury of hindsight, the reader today, with some knowledge of the period under consideration, can see the immediate relevance of the novel perhaps more clearly than the earlier reader could at the time. The biographical problem of the individual author is another variable element. Obviously the personal life, the private experience, of an author is going to influence his ideas, and so his expression of those ideas. Willa Cather, who grew up on the farming frontier, has a different emotional view of isolation from that of Nathaniel Hawthorne, who grew up in a high civilization and had deliberately to seek isolation for himself. The life of Mark Twain, so different from the life of Cooper, produced a different set of assumptions about life in America. Or, again, for any writer of the past the continuing sense of isolation from the popular American culture is another personal element that must be taken into account in his handling of the theme. The lot of the artist in America has generally not been an easy one. There is no one pattern; there is only the sure knowledge that the theme of a great novel is related organically to its time, and for the author its time is in large part made up of his own experiences.

The American novel, too, presents most of the possible situations in the complex relationship of the individual and the group, isolation and society, loneliness and fellow man. Deerslayer, like Daniel Boone, wants nothing to do with others; society and civilization are to be vigorously avoided. So, too, Twain's Huck Finn and Salinger's Holden Caulfield would like to run away from society to the free, isolated life. Theirs would be isolation by choice. Hawthorne's Hester Prynne, on the other hand, like James's Isabel Archer, is isolated against her will and must find some way to regain a meaningful relationship with others. Wolfe's Eugene Gant is a desperately lonely young man lost in the self-pity of his loneliness, like Faulkner's Gail Hightower, as opposed to Faulkner's Joe Christmas, who meets his isolation with rage and fury, or Willa Cather's Ántonia, who meets hers with understanding and acceptance. To take still another set of contrasts, James's Isabel Archer believes in meeting problems

alone, depending only on the inner strength and resistance
of oneself; Steinbeck's Joads believe in the strength and
resistance of the family and hope for the strength of some
larger organized group. Again there is no easy pattern, no
one situation that has caught the imagination of all the
novelists. There cannot be, for the novel grows from life,
and life in America has no one easy pattern to present.

Despite the different sorts of relationship to their times,
the different fictional problems and situations, even the different personal lives of the authors, the novels do show a
surprising agreement with Governor Bradford's early desire
for "much sweet and delightful society and spiritual comfort
together in the ways of God." Even here there are exceptions, of course, such as Cooper's *Deerslayer*. But on the
whole the novels are in agreement with the ideal of the
individual in a spiritual society, man in union with fellow
man in the mutual recognition of ultimate values. But to say
that Bradford's ideal became America's ideal in its novels is
at best a broad generality and at worst misleading. At one
extreme of interpretation is Bradford's literal commonwealth
of God in which the individual is to be subordinated to a
society dedicated to building the new Jerusalem. At the
other extreme might be the Joads' desire for a society
organized for self-protection in a threatening and inhuman
world. These latter would be in a sense political organi-
zations, societies with some ulterior purpose, and the novel
in general is not much interested in them. It is interested,
however, in the general idea of man in "delightful society,"
of the individual united with other individuals for mutual
comfort and loss of isolation in the face of the continual
threat of loneliness and crabbed self-concern.

The conclusion is likely to be misleading too because the
novel as a general rule puts all of its emphasis on the individual; society for most American novels exists only in

relationship to the individuals with whom the particular novel is concerned. This is particularly fitting in a dramatization of the theme of isolation, for loneliness and isolation, however relevant they may be to the whole concept of society in which the individual lives, are by necessity individual problems that man must meet by himself. And so the American novel is concentrated, not on abstract concepts of society or theories of social organization, but on the isolated individual who must work out his problem of isolation for himself. Here Bradford's conclusions furnish the real center of agreement, however widely any single novel may revolve about that center. Bradford, of course, puts his idea in traditional theological terms: to live meaningfully, happily, productively, the individual through the grace of God must live in Christian charity with his fellows, loving his neighbor as himself, and bearing always in mind that the chief end of man is to glorify God and enjoy Him forever. In such a Christian life true loneliness is impossible and isolation is merely a physical condition rather than an emotional one. If certain social and political ideas follow logically, they are important all right, but they are merely derivatives of the greater truth that exists whether man in society puts it into organized group practice or not.

The novel, as befits a literary form considered profane and even ungodly by earlier ages, does not express its theme in such explicitly religious terms. But in its own profane way it agrees with Bradford: man finds the answer to isolation and loneliness by seeking to forget self, by putting love of others before love of self, by losing self in moral commitment that even denies the self. Expressed here in such a baldly didactic way, the conclusion seems stiff and preacher-like. But emerging dramatically from the organic unity of theme, character, story in so many great novels, the conclusion has a constantly increasing impact that is emotionally and

intellectually moving. There is nothing coldly religious about
Isabel Archer's decision to return to her repulsive husband
and defeat her isolation by denying the demands of self. It
is a moving decision by a strong and likable woman. There
is nothing stiffly didactic about Hester Prynne's defeating
the isolation imposed on her by the town in acts of charity
and service to the town. It is emotionally right as well as
theologically right. Governor Bradford might not enjoy the
thought of ungodly novels expressing his ideas, but they are
his ideas after all. Or rather, they are again the ideas inherited
from the experience of all men facing the challenge of isolation and the ideas inherited from the whole religious tradition,
expressed clearly and vigorously by one of the early founders
of the America that produced the novels. There should be
nothing surprising in the agreement; the novelist and the
historian belong to the same tradition and are considering
much the same life.

There are exceptions, of course, but the agreement is
far greater than the disagreement. And the exceptions—*The
Deerslayer*, for instance, and *Look Homeward, Angel*—are
novels that seem more shallow and less satisfactory than the
others. It is now a little unfashionable to speak of the "truth"
of a work of art, and indeed the word in the past was over-
used. The student of literature today prefers to consider the
"truth" of a novel to itself; that is, the inner integrity of a work
of art by which each of its many complex elements works
integrally with all the others to provide one unified whole.
Certainly most of the great novels here do have that sort of
truth. But it is apparent from these novels too that one
element of that final integrity may be a moral truth, a validity
of moral values springing from the experience of life itself.
Whether the final effect is then to be called esthetic or
moral does not seem very important. The important point
here is that many of the greatest American novels do agree on

a moral truth about isolation that all experience has taught
the American: the only way to overcome isolation is to overcome the self by turning outward in what Christianity calls
charity and the American is likely to call more generally
love or sympathy for fellow man. And such an agreement,
despite the occasional exceptions, does suggest that the truth
has a validity outside of the world of these novels as well
as inside. The American knows that it does, and that is one
reason that he has accepted these novels as great American
expressions.

No one example could ever serve as summary of the conclusion of the theme of isolation in the American novel,
much less as summary of the theme itself in all its variety and
richness. Yet one novel seems to tower at the center of the
theme—as it towers at the center of so many other themes—
and to come as near encompassing it as any novel has yet
or is likely to again in the future. Wherever the literary
historian turns in working with the American novel he is
sure sooner or later to meet Herman Melville's *Moby Dick*,
and there seems no stronger way to end the discussion of
the theme of human isolation in the American novel than
to let Melville have the final word of conclusion and summary. Yet one of the exciting things about *Moby Dick* is
its stubborn refusal to fit any neat classification, much less
a conclusion. "To produce a mighty book, you must choose
a mighty theme," [507] [1] says Melville, and he has: the
whale and the industry that grew around him, the problems
of good and evil, the nature of man, fate and free will, the
American character and American life. The novel is so
large that it both satisfies and tantalizes the American mind,
for it takes up many of those questions that have always
puzzled and fascinated the American, yet suggests at the same

[1] Page references are to Herman Melville, *Moby-Dick; or, The Whale*
(New York: Harper and Brothers, 1851).

time most of the different and often conflicting answers that the American has found. The problem of human isolation is no exception, even though Melville does offer for this one theme a more nearly conclusive answer than for many of the others. After all, he was an American too. In one sense *Moby Dick* is, in fact, a culmination of the theme in American fiction, even coming as it does in the middle of the nineteenth century. For the novel is not limited to its century but presses insistently into this one as well. In another sense it is not so much a culmination of the theme as a synthesis of all the views that go to make up the theme. All the questions of other novels about human isolation are at least suggested here, and the reader may work backward or forward from *Moby Dick*, attempting to disentangle the various threads of the theme that go to make the one mighty line.

There is no literal American frontier in *Moby Dick*, although the whaling industry in the newly opened Pacific whaling waters has many of the characteristics of a continental frontier. Here man comes to an unexplored region to better his fortunes, to exploit and to explore, to escape from the settled and civilized regions behind, to fly the American flag over a new and promising territory. Even the occasional touches of jingoism, as when the *Pequod* beats out the German *Jungfrau* to a whale or tricks the French *Rose-Bud* out of ambergris, seem appropriate. Like the open prairie too, the open ocean offers isolation from civilized mankind. Ishmael's description even reminds one of Beret Holm's terror in Rölvaag's novel of isolation on the frontier, *Giants in the Earth:*

Now, in calm weather, to swim in the open ocean is as easy to the practised swimmer as to ride in a spring-carriage ashore. But the awful lonesomeness is intolerable. The intense concentration of self in the middle of such a heartless immensity, my God! who can tell it? Mark, how when sailors in a dead calm bathe in the open sea—mark how closely they hug their ship and only coast along her sides. [461–62]

Such lonesomeness may be terrible, but it may also be desirable, for it is an escape from the pressure of life on the shore. When civilization grows too burdensome to Ishmael he takes to the sea, knowing that there he can breathe a new air uncontaminated by the mass of men, with the open, uninhabited sea stretching out endlessly.

On the ocean too, as on the frontier, Ishmael, like the Deerslayer, is simply a man among other men, one who is accepted for what he is and not for what he has been or what his family is. He is subject to the discipline and the chain of command of the ship, of course—the command that is eventually to destroy the ship and crew—but his subjection is voluntary, and in his isolation from the civilization of the land he is in an equality with his fellows that is not so very different from the equality of the frontier. The novel itself, in fact, is in many ways dedicated to the democratic spirit:

But this august dignity I treat of, is not the dignity of kings and robes, but that abounding dignity which has no robed investiture. Thou shalt see it shining in the arm that wields a pick or drives a spike; that democratic dignity which, on all hands, radiates without end from God; Himself! [127–28]

In choosing the isolation of the sea a man chooses to make of himself what he will and can, not what society would have him be. Here he learns not from man only but from nature itself, "led to think untraditionally and independently; receiving all nature's sweet or savage impressions fresh from her own virgin voluntary and confiding breast." [82] The assumption is not so very different from Cooper's in his idyllic picture of Deerslayer on the frontier, the ideal of the free democratic man unfettered by society, receiving his spirit and his education directly from unspoiled nature. But

Melville is hardly so optimistic or so easily convinced as
Cooper, and this is, after all, a whale ship, not an open forest.
The democratic ideal of the frontier is there in the background, as it was in the American mind of the mid-century,
but it is there to be questioned and examined rather than to
be eagerly and perhaps even naively accepted and put into
fictional practice. The isolation of the sea might be sought
as hopefully as the isolation of the frontier, but the reality
of the one might be as disappointing as the reality that later
novelists discovered of the other. The dream is there in
Moby Dick, but so is the daylight world.

The isolation of Captain Ahab is something altogether
different from the pursuit of a democratic free will. As
captain of the *Pequod* he is by tradition a man set apart from
crew and officers. As a monomaniac intent on the destruction
of the white whale he is set apart from all men as a "grotesque," devoted to a cause that makes allowance for no one
and nothing: " 'Swerve me? The path to my fixed purpose
is laid with iron rails, whereon my soul is grooved to run.' "
[186] In his frenzied search for Moby Dick lies most of the
symbolic meaning of the novel, and the critical interpretations
have been many. But whatever the final interpretation, the
meaning of the white whale for Ahab is clear and frightening:

All that most maddens and torments; all that stirs up the lees of
things; all truth with malice in it; all that cracks the sinews and
cakes the brain; all the subtle demonisms of life and thought; all
evil, to crazy Ahab, were visibly personified, and made practi-
cally assailable in Moby Dick. He piled upon the whale's white
hump the sum of all the general rage and hate felt by his whole
race from Adam down; and then, as if his chest had been a
mortar, he burst his hot heart's shell upon it. [203]

In the face of such gigantic madness there is nothing to say;
Ahab is so lost to mankind that to talk of isolation is to talk
in absurd understatement. He would believe that he is the

champion of mankind, the mighty individual heroically riding against the single enemy. But in reality he is pursuing a monomaniac desire for revenge that is so frenzied, so intense, so self-centered, so completely blind to others that he exists only for his hatred. He has no relationship to other men; for him there is only Ahab and Moby Dick, and one must destroy the other.

As captain of the *Pequod*, however, Ahab is placed in a position of responsibility to others, and one of the tragic lessons of the novel is in the sight of his refusal of the responsibilities and the relationships that cannot be refused. When he will not hunt for oil—the purpose of the voyage for all except him—his offense is venial. But when he carries his crew with him to destruction—the crew that is his responsibility—the offense is venal and shows the unforgivable nature of his isolation. The crew of the *Pequod* is international, and the various origins of the men suggest that the ship represents mankind in general: "Yes, the world's a ship on its passage out. . . ." [43] Pagans and Christians, the savage and the civilized, European and American, black and white are all present. When Ahab bends them to his own purpose and takes them down with him he is a man destroying mankind thoughtlessly and carelessly for his own selfish purposes. The analogy of the dictator destroying his nation for a whim, of a Napoleon slaughtering the mankind of Europe, must come to mind as the story of mad Ahab unfolds. When at the beginning of the final chase Ahab says to his mates, " 'Ye two are all mankind; and Ahab stands alone among the millions of the peopled earth, nor gods nor men his neighbors,' " [610] it might with some lonely man have been a touching and pathetic moment. With Ahab, looking back, it is a moment of terrible truth that is to lead to the destruction of his ship and crew as well as of himself.

The horror of Ahab's isolation from man is a double one then: his mad single-minded devotion to one end in life, and his resulting complete indifference to the mankind about him, to the very men for whom he had a responsibility greater than any usual moral responsibility. The result is a complete spiritual isolation that is terrifying in its proportions. In a sense it is terrifying for Ahab too. Just once or twice the reader catches a fragmentary glimpse of the man Ahab might have been:

"What is it, what nameless, inscrutable, unearthly thing is it; what cozzening, hidden lord and master, and cruel, remorseless emperor commands me; that against all natural lovings and longings, I so keep pushing, and crowding, and jamming myself on all the time; recklessly making me ready to do what in my own proper, natural heart, I durst not so much as dare?" [599–600]

But the glimpses are momentary, and Ahab is soon back in his driving madness. At best he is, as Ishmael once thinks, a Prometheus; "a vulture feeds upon that heart for ever; that vulture the very creature he creates." [224] If Ahab does have his "humanities" that sometimes surprise him, he ruthlessly suppresses them. For he has set himself a goal, one final smash at the pasteboard mask over the malignity of the world, and all else must give way before it. In the face of his rage man is of no importance, and the "humanities" of even less. Even he is of no importance except as an agent of revenge. His manhood now is only a ghost dimly suspected, and he only an iron lance of energy aimed at Moby Dick.

The isolation of Ahab is particularly striking too, for he is seen through the eyes of Ishmael, a man commonplace enough to provide dramatic contrast. The contrast is perhaps not always as apparent as it might be, for the shock effect of Ahab is so great that the reader easily forgets that Ishmael is the narrator and is always in control of the reader's view.

At second glance, however, it is readily apparent that it is the very normality of Ishmael that conditions the effect of Ahab and makes him seem so gigantically out of the normal and ordinary, so much the lone, mighty individual. For Ishmael is a likable, recognizable fellow who does not particularly impress the imagination. He occasionally is down in the dumps and moody, as anyone is, but soon is back in his usual cheerful frame of mind, cracking jokes and looking at the world about him with considerable amusement. One cannot even imagine him lost in the mad rage of an Ahab or sullenly feeding upon his gloom. He rather likes to play the part occasionally and think of himself as a misanthropist disillusioned with the world, but the mood is difficult to keep up, and he soon lapses back into cheerfulness. At the same time he is no fool. He has a considerable sensitivity to thought and to human emotion, and he likes to think about the events around him, trying to arrive at the truth behind them. From even the smallest incidents of the voyage he is likely to derive some "moral" that he feels sums up a truth of man or nature. It is an ironic element of the contrast with Ahab that the more Ahab thinks the more he is driven into himself and alienated from the world; the more Ishmael thinks the more he simply comes to understand the world and man. As Ahab says of himself, he never thinks, " 'he only feels, feels, feels; *that's* tingling enough for mortal man!' " [622] It is ironic, once the reader comes to notice it, how much of the real thought of the novel is that given to Ishmael. He is the "commonplace" narrator who makes the reader feel that he is seeing a real world, if not a familiar one, yet at the same time he is intellectually the deepest diver of the novel. Real intelligence and thought, it would seem, do not drive a man into mad isolation.

Ishmael provides a sharp thematic contrast to Ahab too in his feeling of kinship and mutual involvement with mankind. Here the first chapters of the novel are particularly revealing, as they are for so many other themes of the novel. Ishmael, feeling momentarily at odds with the world, is thrown quite literally into the same bed with Queequeg, the pagan harpooner. After the first fright, one of the finest pieces of comedy in the novel, the acquaintance turns soon into genuine friendship as the two search together for berths and finally ship out on the *Pequod*. When Ishmael thinks of the new friendship he sees the change that it has brought about in him: "I felt a melting in me. No more my splintered heart and maddened hand were turned against the wolfish world. This soothing savage had redeemed it." [56] The overstatement is typical; Ishmael is in one of his moods when he purports to find the world wolfish. But the idea is valid for him—and the overstatement makes it ironically applicable to the plight of Ahab yet to be seen—for friendship with man, a turning out from himself, make the world bearable for Ishmael and bring him into a saving relationship with mankind. Here the contrast with Ahab is absolute, for Ahab has no friendships, wants none, can allow himself none. He must stand alone, for friendship demands concern for others, and his chosen isolation denies any concern outside of himself and his hatred.

The contrast of a desirable concern for others finds its clearest statement in the chapter called "The Monkey-Rope." There Ishmael on the deck of the whaler is tied by a line, the monkey-rope, to Queequeg down on the whale in the water below. His job is to save Queequeg from any slip or fall; and if one goes, both go. Ishmael recognizes what Bradford's age would have called the "type" or "emblem":

So strongly and metaphysically did I conceive of my situation then, that while earnestly watching his motions, I seemed distinctly to perceive that my own individuality was now merged in a joint stock company of two: that my free will had received a mortal wound; and that another's mistake or misfortune might plunge innocent me into unmerited disaster and death. . . . I saw that this situation of mine was the precise situation of every mortal that breathes; only, in most cases, he, one way or other, has this Siamese connexion with a plurality of other mortals. [356]

Man cannot escape his connections with man; to try to deny them is the way of madness, and to try to ignore them is the way to inevitable destruction. But Ahab is mad, and inevitably he is destroyed, taking others with him in ironic illustration of the truth he ignores. In his complete isolation from man he cannot or will not even read the lesson being acted out on his own ship.

Ishmael's sense of humanity, of participation in the lot of mankind, comes from a deeper sense than that of observation and deduction from experience. With a half-smile he speaks of being "born and bred in the bosom of the infallible Presbyterian Church." [58] And then he goes on to say that this does not prohibit his respecting Queequeg's idolatry, and even worshiping with him: "But what is worship?—to do the will of God?—*that* is worship. And what is the will of God?—to do to my fellow man what I would have my fellow man to do to me—*that* is the will of God." [58] His belief is nothing unusual, nor is it out of keeping with his role as the commonplace narrator that even William Dean Howells might later have recognized. Early in the novel, while he is still almost tragically innocent, he can go so far as to say— although with a little deliberate sarcasm—that "a man's religion is one thing, and this practical world quite another." [83] But even in his commonplace faith he is in startling contrast to Ahab, who has dashed his heavenly quadrant with his earthly. In what Starbuck calls "his heaven-insulting purpose," [187] Ahab has not only abandoned Christianity and its view of man, he has turned blasphemously against it.

When Christian rites appear on his ship, they are monstrous distortions, as in the parody of the communion when he forces his harpooners to drink to the death of Moby Dick from the sockets of their harpoons. If the Christian God enters his thought at all, it is only as an opponent or as something to be swept aside from the path to his revenge. There is even the suggestion that he has replaced Christianity with a form of fire worship, with Fedallah as his familiar in the magic rites, reflecting the fire constantly burning within his own soul. Even his name is fitting: Ahab, the king of Israel who deserted Jehovah to worship Baal. With such a captain, lost to humanity and to faith, the fate of the crew is determined before they sail, and the prophecies of death and destruction seem only fitting.

The suggestion of magic, of fire worship, of prophecy belong to what might be called in general the romantic element of the story. But the constant emphasis on religion belongs to the novel as a whole, realistic and romantic and symbolic as well, and is at the heart of the novel. It finds its clearest statement in Father Mapple's sermon before the beginning of the voyage; the rest of the book is to be seen in relationship to that sermon. There Father Mapple tells the story of Jonah, the story that is relevant in so many ways to the story of *Moby Dick*. His conclusion, in which he offers in one of the finest rhetorical passages of the novel the topgallant delight of active and steadfast faith and of unselfish devotion to God, is to color the rest of the work, for it offers a positive statement of truth against which character and action may be measured. To miss the point is to miss the full effect of the novel. The definition of the sin of Jonah might have been aimed directly at Ahab himself:

"As with all sinners among men, the sin of this son of Amittai was in his wilful disobedience of the command of God . . . which he found a hard command. But all the things that God would have us do are hard for us to do—remember that—and hence, he oftener commands us than endeavors to persuade. And if we obey God, we must disobey ourselves; and it is in this disobeying ourselves, wherein the hardness of obeying God consists." [45–46]

This, then, is the failure of Ahab; he cannot disobey himself. As Ishmael later notes, "With little external to constrain us, the innermost necessities in our being, these still drive us on." [182] And Ahab has nothing outside of his hatred to constrain him. He is an isolated man given a position of command with no religious, moral, or humanitarian limitations to check him, and his inner compulsions can drive him to his own and others' destruction.

At the center of Ahab's story this conflict of the self with concern for something other than the self is dramatically fought out. Ironically, or perhaps fittingly, Father Mapple helps to define some of the difficulties of the problem: " 'Delight is to him—a far, far upward, and inward delight—who against the proud gods and commodores of this earth, ever stands forth his own inexorable self.' " [53] At first glance the implied definition of the self would seem to agree with Ahab's definition: assertion, courage, power, the refusal to bow to anything outside. These qualities Ahab has, and they make him an awesome figure, satanically heroic in his proportions, the one mighty individual. Although he cannot command the approval of men, he can and does command the admiration; his very conviction and undaunted determination are humanly impressive to commonplace men. Starbuck, with his "mere unaided virtue or right-mindedness," [206] cannot stand up against the force of Ahab's self, and the reader can understand why. There is something of the hero of the older imagination, something larger than life, to Ahab, and his exploits and battles can only be watched with apprehensive passivity. Certainly there can be no disagreement with one of his final vaunts: " 'In the midst of the personified impersonal, a personality stands here.' " [560] The very pride is a part of the personality and in keeping with an older heroic tradition. To Ahab his is the only self of importance; all else must give way before it. He alone is the champion of the earth, and he must live and fight in isolation from petty man. The " 'grand, ungodly, god-like man, Captain Ahab' " [89] must and will exert the full force of his personality to achieve his own ends, and this for him is the greatest mark and the highest definition of the self.

There is another form of the "own inexorable self" in the novel, however, and one that is not, like Milton's Satan, so mixed in its effect, one milder and less awesomely impressive yet eventually stronger and more lasting. When Ishmael is first looking for a berth he thinks of the indignities and the loss of pride that he will have to endure:

Well, then, however the old sea-captains may order me about— however they may thump and punch me about, I have the satisfaction of knowing that it is all right; that everybody else is one way or other served in much the same way—either in a physical or metaphysical point of view, that is; and so the universal thump is passed round, and all hands should rub each other's shoulder-blades, and be content. [5]

Pride of self to Ishmael is not merely a matter of the unchecked assertion of self. As always, he sees himself in relation to others, and knows that he is, after all, only a man like other men and must participate in the common lot, tied as he is to the mutual monkey-rope. And even within the individual self, insofar as it can be distinguished from the common self of man, other values are to be sought than the power to force man and nature to conform to his own will. While considering, of all unlikely things for such consideration, the structure of the whale Ishmael points out the emblem to be read there:

It does seem to me, that herein we see the rare virtue of a strong individual vitality, and the rare virtue of thick walls, and the rare virtue of interior spaciousness. Oh, man! admire and model thyself after the whale! Do thou, too, remain warm among ice. Do thou, too, live in this world without being of it. Be cool at the equator; keep thy blood fluid at the Pole. Like the great dome of St. Peter's, and like the great whale, retain, O man! in all seasons a temperature of thine own. [343]

Ishmael too would turn within for a consistency that makes the self, but it is a consistency of something quite different from Ahab's self.

While floating in the midst of a pod of whales, Ishmael sees the analogue of his own hidden life, the heart of his self:

But even so, amid the tornadoed Atlantic of my being, do I myself still for ever centrally disport in mute calm; and while ponderous planets of unwaning woe revolve round me, deep down and deep inland there I still bathe me in eternal mildness of joy. [433]

Here is the deepest contrast between Ishmael and Ahab, the eternal mildness of joy against the burning pride of hatred. Joy is within and is a deep consistency, even like Ahab's hatred, but it arises from a knowledge of the humanity of the self and from a dependence on man and a trust in God. This is the commonplace, human equivalent of that topgallant delight that Father Mapple promises to him " 'whom all the waves of the billows of the seas of the boisterous mob can never shake from this sure Keel of the Ages.' " [53] This is the humility of dependence rather than the pride of independence. Now, Ishmael is no saint, of course; his inner joy and peace are only a weakly human approximation of the ultimate joy. But he is in clear contrast to Ahab, who has rejected the idea itself of joy, and he provides the necessary balance to Ahab's overbalanced understanding of the "own inexorable self." For Ahab satisfies only one part of Father Mapple's demand for the self; he stands immensely against the powers of the earth, but he does not stand for any power not of his self. Ishmael, for all of his human frailty and his commonplace position, would give the self a greater meaning and eventually a greater strength; he would stand for humanity and for God as well as against "the proud gods and commodores of this earth." The strength of his self does not need to come from within only but gathers greater strength from without to add to that within.

It is fitting as well as necessary (the necessities of this novel are all fitting in the final pattern) that Ishmael is the one man to survive the final disaster and return to the world of men to tell the story. Ahab had never belonged to the world of men, but Ishmael is clearly of it and belongs to others as well as to himself. Perhaps it is fate that determines this end, for the novel allows the possibility at least. Ahab is convinced: " 'This whole act's immutably decreed. 'Twas rehearsed by thee and me a billion years before this ocean rolled. Fool! I am the Fates' lieutenant; I act under orders.' " [620] But Ahab would think so, for he believes himself a man set apart from common man for some inevitable heroic role. And if he is not caught in the balance of dependence and responsibility with other men, he must explain the outside forces at work on him in some fashion. He rejects God, so only fate is left. All is in keeping with the isolation that marks the man. Ishmael characteristically is not so sure and thinks of fate in more human terms. The chapter called "The Mat-Maker" offers the culmination of one line of his thought as he notes in the mat being woven an analogue of fate, chance, and free will meeting to weave the fabric of life. And even this analogy shows less awareness of humanity than we ordinarily associate with Ishmael, and less awareness of the Christian view of life. But the small inconsistencies of Ishmael's conclusions are themselves marks of his humanity and set him in contrast to Ahab, who in his isolation is almost inhumanly sure of himself and his beliefs.

Ishmael, after all, is only a man like other men. His often skeptical air even makes him seem not unlike the commonplace man of this century, and one comment sums up the impression that he gives in his narration to the entire novel: "Doubts of all things earthly, and intuitions of some things heavenly; this combination makes neither believer nor infidel, but makes a man who regards them both with equal eye." [416] Ahab, in his very absence of doubts, has seized one truth, in almost complete fulfillment of Sherwood Anderson's definition of the "grotesque," and made it the whole truth for him. In his mind there is no room for doubt or for allowances, and so there can be no participation in a common humanity that is plagued with doubts and must constantly make allowances. And then the one overriding truth, the one explanation of man and the world that can satisfy man and give him a truth to hold to without making him a grotesque, Ahab rejects. Ishmael has flashes of the truth at least, enkindling his fog, as he says, with a heavenly ray, to save him from the dark madness of an Ahab. He can be humanly sympathetic with Ahab's own acceptance of a limited truth—at one point in his innocence he can even say, "Ahab's quenchless feud seemed mine" [196]—but never so lost to the world or to God as to believe that he alone has found all of the truth.

Father Mapple may withdraw to the physical isolation of his pulpit—ironically in the form of a ship—to signify spiritual withdrawal from worldly ties, but it is only for contemplation and for necessary detachment. His message is for all men and for the world. And it is a message that calls down through American history and the American novel to the common concern of Americans with the problem of human isolation. A few men may seek physical isolation for just such freedom from the pressures of civilization, from the social and economic and moral distortions that man in the mass has created for himself. This is the freedom of the frontier, and it is a tempting promise, whatever its fulfillment may be in reality. But most men must live with other men, and the threat of spiritual isolation is always there. Here his answer is the same answer that others have found before and after him: man, even the mighty individual, must reach outside of himself in some mutual relationship that will defeat the pride of self. For Father Mapple, as for Governor Bradford, the final answer is in faith and dependence on God, in the loss of self to the greater truth of God. In *Moby Dick* this is the ultimate truth that underlies all. Although Ishmael catches glimmerings of the truth, he sees it most clearly in one of its related truths that John Steinbeck in his different fashion was later to insist on: the mutual dependence of man in his weakness and the necessity of recognizing and accepting the dependence. There is no need for organization or for outward gestures, as in Steinbeck's novel; there is simply need for acceptance of the fact. Ishmael does accept it, and he can live among men. Ahab can never accept it, for in his fatal pride he finds all his strength and all his being within himself. He has made his self his own god. When something challenges this self, call it fate or the malignancy of the world or just Moby Dick, he can only strike out against it. The result is a personal courage and a tortured heroism that thrills the imagination. But the result is also an overbearing pride and a destructive monomania that repels and a spiritual isolation so terrible and so complete that it appalls.

Here in Ahab is the giant personality that so often marks the great novels of his age. But it is a personality in isolation, and one that never has the final strength to defeat its isolation. Hester Prynne and Isabel Archer, perhaps even Huckleberry Finn, are in their different and less rhetorical ways giant personalities too. But if they do not so immediately impress the imagination with their stature, they are nevertheless stronger individuals than Ahab, for they can defeat the pride that threatens the strong personality and can defeat the isolation that accompanies pride. In *Moby Dick* it is Ishmael who survives in the humility and the sense of humanity that he has learned. If he is a commonplace man who is not so very different from the characters of a Howells or a Steinbeck or even a Faulkner yet to come, he is still the stronger man than Ahab, and eventually the victorious man. He is the final answer of so many great American novels to the insistently pressing problem of spiritual isolation, the answer first suggested by Governor Bradford: the defeat of pride of self, the reaching out in humility or in charity from the hollowness within, the escape from the dungeon of the heart, the full acceptance of one's being simply a man among dependent men.

Index